Hypnotherapy Inductions and Deepenings
Volume I

By:

Steve G. Jones, M.Ed.
Clinical Hypnotherapist
www.SteveGJones.com

Research Assistant: Katherine T. Sinclair

Copyright © 2007

ISBN 978-0-6151-6731-2

Table of Contents

Foreword

In the 1950s, the American Medical Association took notice of hypnosis after a patient underwent a thyroidectomy (removal of the thyroid) while in a hypnotic trance induced by a hypnotherapist (Blakeslee, 2005). No other painkiller or anesthesia was used.

Since then, hypnotherapists have made powerful strides toward changing public perception about hypnosis. Doctors continue to use hypnosis to calm their patients, and to ease pain during procedures (Bierman, 1995). They regularly tell patients how easy recovery will be. Additionally, doctors tell patients that a procedure is common and meets with a high degree of success. Because these phrases are delivered by an authority figure, they act in exactly the same way as hypnotic suggestions, and become reality for the patient. More obvious hypnotic suggestions are also sometimes given to patients by doctors trained in hypnosis, and for over a century, dentists have used hypnosis to ease discomfort during dental procedures.

In addition to using hypnotic techniques themselves, doctors and dentists regularly refer patients to hypnotherapists for help with weight loss, smoking cessation, and overcoming fears about dental and surgical procedures. Before the 1950s, the medical profession scoffed at hypnotherapy, but today it is being readily embraced as a complement to long-standing medical procedures.

According to the Southern Medical Journal (2004), as many as 40% of Americans use some form of complementary and alternative medicine such as hypnotherapy. At no other time has the world of hypnotherapy been as wide open with exciting possibilities as it is now. Because more and more people are exploring and accepting the benefits of hypnotherapy, a much greater need for qualified hypnotherapists to open practices now exists. The goal of this book is to give you — a potential or practicing hypnotherapist — a strong base for building your practice. You will be guided through a basic hypnotherapy session, and you will be given homework opportunities to use and modify your techniques so that you can help others lose weight, find love, and increase their financial success, among other issues.

For the latest information about the hypnotherapy world, visit www.americanallianceofhypnotists.org the website of the American Alliance of Hypnotists, of which I am the founder and director. The organization started in America as a network of hypnotherapists, but it is now open to practitioners worldwide. Among other things, this site lists hypnotherapists and classes available in your local area. Become a member. It's free.

Chapter 1

About Inductions

Steve G. Jones, M.Ed.

An induction is the tool that hypnotherapists use to induce hypnosis. It marks the beginning of hypnosis (and the beginning of the recording you will make for your clients). Inductions come in all shapes and sizes. This chapter will focus on inductions that are simple yet effective.

Relaxation Inductions

The basic induction is called a "relaxation induction." With a relaxation induction, you want to bore a person into the Alpha state. Imagine talking to someone and trying to bore her. Some people are able to do this naturally. Some people will start talking, and their listeners immediately get a glazed-over look in their eyes. That type of speaker would be an excellent hypnotherapist. If you are one of those people, congratulations! Now you can help others with your natural ability to bore.

Have you ever been in a classroom with a teacher who talked incessantly with a monotone voice because she has taught the same subject for years and had no passion left in her entire being? That may have actually done you some good. Although you could not consciously pay attention, you may have processed some of the information hypnotically. I guarantee you that the teacher was lulling you into a trance.

Watching TV will lull you into a trance. Driving a car will lull you into a trance. A slow-talking, monotonous teacher speaking for 45 minutes will definitely lull you into a trance.

During a relaxation induction, speak in a monotone voice. Stretch out your words. Speak slowly and methodically and enunciate clearly.

When working with the subconscious mind, you must be very careful that you say *exactly* what you mean. The subconscious mind will take things literally. Any time you are working with someone under hypnosis, speak very clearly. Make sure that she can understand every word. Act as though your patient is a foreigner and does not speak your language very well. You need to speak slowly and clearly so that there is no misunderstanding, because if you pronounce a word incorrectly, the subconscious mind may process it as another word.

Practice saying the phrase, "Jack and Jill went up the hill." Stretch out the words, especially the word "and." Practice this until it is as relaxing (i.e., boring) as possible. This is the only time in your life when being boring is a good thing. If you are not sure of the tone of voice that you should use, visit www.SteveGJones.com. Any of the CDs there will serve as an excellent example.

It is important to refer to the five senses during the induction. Most people relate strongly to one of the senses: sight, touch, hearing, smell, or taste. I like to involve as many of the other senses as possible.

By involving *all* the senses, you can get to the one that the client relates most strongly with. Make sure that the induction has something for the client to see, to feel, to hear, to taste, and to smell. If you have already determined that the client relates strongly to one particular sense, reference that sense more often than the others in your induction. But use all of the senses with everyone to make a well-rounded induction every time.

Let me illustrate this point by taking you through an induction. Because the purpose of the induction is to slow the person down, you should also play soft, calming music in the background.

(Feel free to use verbatim any of the hypnosis session material I provide in this book.)

All right now. I want you to take a deep breath in through your nose, inhaling very slowly, filling your lungs and stretching them out. That's right. Hold it. Open your mouth slightly and exhale very slowly, and as you do, just feel your body relaxing, relaxing, relaxing. Good. Now to help you to relax, I want you to visualize yourself on a beautiful beach. It is your beach. You are relaxed and safe. You are walking along the beach. Feel the warm, soft sand on your feet. Feel the warmth of the sun relaxing every part of your body. Inhale the scent of the sea air. Feel the relaxing breeze blowing gently across your body as you walk slowly down to the water, where the waves are making a relaxing sound.

Let's break this down. First of all, having people breathe in and out slowly is going to relax them. (Many people who are addicted to cigarettes are simply addicted to the idea of taking deep, relaxing breaths. They are taking the time to take a deep breath, hold it, and blow it out. Taking a "smoker's break" allows the smoker to take a break, go outside, and stop working. Everything shuts down while the smoker takes deep, yogic breaths and blows them out. Unfortunately, the smoker is also inhaling 4,000 chemicals.)

Your client will take three or four deep breaths in and out. Just relax the person and get her to slow down.

Let's now take a look at the rest of the induction.

I want you to visualize yourself on a beautiful beach. Here, I am referring to the client's sense of sight.

<u>You are walking along the beach.</u> This is the kinetic (movement) aspect. I have engaged the feelings of motion and have offered something to those people who relate strongly to motion.

<u>Feel the warm, soft sand on your feet.</u> Now I have engaged tactile listeners. Notice that I did not just say, "You are feeling the sand." I described the sand. I made it real. The sand feels warm. It feels soft. (You may even say the sand is white, which again involves the visual sense.) I grew up in South Florida, so I can relate strongly to this experience. I have been on the beach many times, and that sand is warm, if not hot. That brings back a clear memory for me. Most people have walked barefooted on a beach in the daytime. Be sure to use something that is familiar to a wide variety of people.

<u>Feel the warmth of the sun relaxing every part of your body.</u> Again, I am referring to the sense of feeling, also called touch or the tactile sense. I've also linked the feeling to something relaxing.

<u>Inhale the scent of the sea air.</u> Here, I have prompted the olfactory sense, appealing to the sense of smell. Most people know exactly the smell I mean when I say "sea air."

<u>Feel the relaxing breeze blowing gently across your body.</u> Here I am using the tactile sense (the sense of touch).

<u>As you walk slowly down to the water.</u> The client is moving. Again, I am engaging the kinetic (motion) sense.

It is important to engage all of the senses because some people relate strongly to just one sense. Some people are very visual. For example, in their mind's eye, they will see the beach clearly. They will fill the ocean with sailboats, put buildings on the land in the distance, and add a few clouds in the beautiful blue sky.

Others do not see anything. They will listen to that exact same induction, and they will have a nonvisual sense of being on the beach. They will have the feeling that they are on the beach because they can feel it on the soles of their feet. Or they just somehow sense that they are there. Maybe the smell, the scent of the sea air draws them in.

Unless you want to get into an extensive (and unnecessary) pretest to determine which sense the client favors, cover every sense. Even if you know that the client relates strongly to motion, add the other sensory elements; doing so will more fully engage her. You want to make sure that the client hears a description of all the things people typically experience at the beach.

By the way, if your client is afraid of water or of beaches for any reason, you should use a different induction. Ask the client ahead of time if she likes the beach!

Remember to be sensitive to each of your clients. If you are writing an induction for someone in a wheelchair, do not describe how the client is walking along the beach or rolling her wheelchair along the sandy beach. Choose another scenario for the induction. If you are talking about swimming and your client cannot swim, then she is not going to have a relaxing experience. Ask the client ahead of time about her abilities, likes, and dislikes.

Inductions should incorporate the types of experiences that the person enjoys. For instance, if you are hypnotizing a scuba diver, your inductions might be about a dive. Think about the possibilities. The client is going down, down, deeper and deeper. Maybe the client likes to go driving in the desert. She could imagine the drive in the Mojave Desert at night with the top down on a convertible. Stay open and creative.

If someone is coming to you for a few sessions, you may not want to use the same induction every time. You might want to mix it up.

Once, when I was doing a diving induction, I said, "And now you take a deep breath in through your nose and out through your mouth." Divers wear regulators in their mouths to get air from the tank. They do not breathe through their noses while diving! They breathe through the mouth.

After the session, the client said, "You know, that was great and relaxing, except for when you told me to breathe in through my nose and out through my mouth."

I was not thinking of what the patient was experiencing. Instead, I was looking at the client in the chair and thinking that she should breathe through her nose. In her mind, she was scuba diving. The mind makes it real for the body. She was there, and I was incongruent.

Make sure that you plan ahead of time *and* think on your feet.

At the same time, do not be afraid to make mistakes. I have been doing hypnosis for a long time, and I still make mistakes. Be aware of the ramifications, and if the mistake is a bad one, do what you can to fix it in a calm way. Sometimes, the mistakes are not as bad as you think they are, or the person does not even notice it. In this case, do not point out the mistake.

In fact, a mistake could be used as a confusion induction, which is covered in the next section.

Know that the rules are flexible. Think about it like dancing at a club. There is freedom of expression. Are the rules set in stone? No. You can be flexible. Do no harm, fix mistakes, but be flexible. Try things with the best of intentions and flex your muscles, and I guarantee that you will grow.

If something does not work, try something else. The person may report, "I just could not get into that. I was not relaxed." What should you do?

First, assure the client that even in Alpha, a person is up to 200 times more suggestible.

Second, make a change. You may think, "Okay, the beach induction is not working on this woman. She likes the city sounds. I do not like them, in fact I find them annoying, but that does not matter because she likes them. She is going to get them."

The following is an example of a short induction script.

And you find yourself driving along the Pacific Coast Highway now. You are headed north, leaving Los Angeles. You are in a convertible and enjoying the breeze in your hair. You see the relaxing ocean to your left. And you see the high cliffs to your upper right. And the more you drive, the more you relax. You see birds overhead, and smell that salty sea air as you continue to drive down the road. You are safe and protected. Sometimes, it seems as though the car drives itself. You are relaxing more and more as you drive. And as I am silent now, just allow yourself to enjoy the beautiful day and relax more deeply.

That's right, just relaxing and drifting as you drive down the road in your convertible. Enjoying the beautiful day. And as you now look in the rearview mirror, you realize just how far down the road you have driven. And it occurs to you that you are very relaxed.

Sample Induction 1

You're in your car; it's afternoon; it's early spring. You're driving on a smooth, curving road that leads through the hillside. The grass is vividly green, and colorful wild flowers are in bloom on the sides of the road. There are trees lush with leaves. The air is fresh and clean. You feel yourself begin to relax. The road curves gently to the right, and your car hugs the curves of the road as if it were on a track. The mist in the air rises and clears as you drive. You feel the warm air against your skin as your car follows the road. You notice that your car is the only one on the road. The engine of your car purring gently is the only sound. It's quiet. It's safe. You haven't a care in the world; you are at peace, enjoying the beautiful scenery as you drive. The sky is blue and it is clear, but for a few wisps of clouds. You are so comfortable and serene. You're driving slowly, taking in the beautiful scenery.

You approach a gravel road. It calls to you, so you turn onto it. You hear the light crunching of the tires on the finely ground gravel. The road leads through a wooded area. The sun filters through the trees; it is warm and bright. There is beauty all around you and you take it all in. You come to the end of the road. It is large and circular. You see a clearing and a path and you park your car close to the clearing. The car door closes gently as you walk toward the trail. As you approach the trail, you notice that it is wide and carpeted with the same fine gravel as on the road. As you walk past the trees, you hear some birds singing. You walk slowly, taking in all the sights and smells. You see a honeysuckle bush, and you stop and smell the flowers. You pick a flower. The flower smells so sweet and the honeysuckle tastes like honey. You savor the taste and continue on the path.

You hear the gurgling of water nearby. As you continue on the trail, the gravel path turns to grass, and there are stepping-stones that lead to a waterfall. You take off your shoes and carry them along with you. There are beautiful purple and yellow flowers on either side of the trail. The stepping-stones feel smooth and warm on your feet. Each stone is a different color of the stone rainbow. As you step on each stone on the path, you become more relaxed. The stones are beautiful. Each step relaxes you more. You continue on the stepping-stones, relaxing more with each step. You are getting closer to the waterfall. The waterfall ends in a calm, clear pool of water. You set your shoes aside on a rock near the pool. You put your toe in the water to test the temperature. You find it warm and inviting. You wade into the pool and find a large rock to sit on. You sit down on the rock. You put your hand in the water and move it slowly back and forth, feeling the warmth of the water between your fingers and around your hand.

You take a deep breath through your nose. You can taste the freshness of the air as your chest rises and your lungs fill with the clean air. You open your mouth slightly and exhale slowly. You take another slow, deep breath through your nose, and again exhale slowly though your mouth. Once again, another slow, deep breath. The water gently falls into the pool and ripples in the water traveling slowly toward you. You watch the ripples of the water and become more relaxed as each ripple floats by you. Two purple dragonflies hover on the water. They linger a few minutes and then fly off. They take with them any cares and anxieties that may have remained. You take another deep breath and feel so calm, so relaxed.

You look around and see a hammock hanging between two trees. You slowly lift yourself out of the pool and walk toward the hammock. The hammock is covered with a large pillow that perfectly fits the hammock. You easily get into the hammock. The hammock supports you effortlessly. You feel as if you're floating in the softness of the hammock. The trees filter the warm sun and you feel safe, comfortable, supported. You close your eyes and rest your mind.

Sample Induction 2

Now close your eyes. Take a nice, deep, full breath and exhale slowly. Take another deep breath and exhale. Feel yourself beginning to relax now … from the very top of your head … all the way down … to the very tip of your toes. One more time. Breathe in. Take a nice, deep, full breath and hold it in. Now let it out completely, and feel yourself relaxing even more.

I want you to imagine now that you are looking at a clear, blue sky. It is a brilliant blue, like no other color you have ever seen. And in the sky, a sky-writing airplane is writing your name in fluffy, white, cloud-like letters. See your name floating …fluffy, white and cloud-like in a clear, blue sky. Reach out and imagine what the clouds feel like. Light and airy. Also, hear the birds. Not only can you hear their calls, but you can also hear the flapping of their wings as they increase their speed. You hear the silence of their wings as they glide through the sky. You relax with the increasing silence.

Now let your name just disappear with the wind. Let the winds just blow your name away into the blue of the sky … and forget about your name. Forget you even have a name. Names are not important. Just go on listening to my voice and let yourself relax even more. You no longer hear or see the birds. You are at complete peace with yourself. There are no distractions. You relax even deeper.

Helpful Tip

As you write inductions and deepenings (next chapter), you need to use your creativity. Try keeping a pocket recorder or note pad and pen handy. Perhaps a great idea for an induction/deepening will come to you in the grocery store, in the shower, or when you just get up in the morning. You never know when a brilliant idea might come.

Suggested Practice

Write your own induction. Do not spend a lot of time laboring over this — just let your creativity flow and write it out. It can be one page or 10 pages, though it should be no more than 10 minutes long when read aloud. Have the client walk along the beach, or in the woods, or in any other place that is relaxing and peaceful. Incorporate all the senses. Remember when reading it to pronounce everything perfectly so that there is no misunderstanding.

Record the induction on a computer (mp3 file or CD). Then listen to it and see if it bores you. It should. See if it relaxes you. See if it gets you into that altered state of mind. See if it drops you into Alpha, where you are just a little bit slower, just a little bit more relaxed than you normally are when fully awake. And if it puts you completely to sleep and you wake up a couple of hours later, that is fine.

Between each section of the recorded hypnotherapy session, insert 30 to 60 seconds of silence. This aids in relaxing the client. If you have gentle, soothing music playing in the background, continue to play it during the silent periods. Like everything else you do in this book, you will use this induction over and over, so make it outstanding!

Caution: Do not ever listen to your induction or anything hypnotic in a moving vehicle.

Test Your Knowledge on Chapter 1 - Inductions
(See back of book for correct answers)

- **Question 1**

Write one sentence, which, when used in an induction, would involve the sense of touch (tactile sense).

- **Question 2**

Write one sentence, which, when used in an induction, would involve the sense of smell (olfactory sense).

- **Question 3**

Write one sentence, which, when used in an induction, would involve the sense of sight (visual sense).

- **Question 4**

Write one sentence, which, when used in an induction, would involve the sense of sound (auditory sense).

- **Question 5**

Why is it important to speak slowly and clearly in a hypnotherapy session?

Steve G. Jones, M.Ed.

Chapter 2

About Deepenings

Steve G. Jones, M.Ed.

A deepening varies only slightly from an induction. In fact, the terms *deepening* and *induction* are often interchanged. Strictly speaking, however, a deepening comes after an induction and before a script. The purpose of the deepening, as the name implies, is to drop the patient into a deeper state of consciousness.

After the induction, the patient is relaxed, comfortable, and peaceful. Now that you have the patient under your control, so to speak, you want to relax him even more. To do so, you will take your patient down something such as a set of stairs, an elevator, or an escalator.

I like to have several inductions with accompanying deepenings. This is for two reasons. First, clients coming in for several sessions like to hear different inductions and deepenings. Second, occasionally you will have clients who do not like several of your induction/deepening combinations. It is better to have several from which to choose.

Overkill is not necessary. When I first started using hypnosis in 1983, I had people go down miles of stairs. If your patient is reasonably relaxed, two short stairways (of ten steps each) are plenty. There is no need to give your client a workout. Confine your deepening to 10 units (e.g., stairs) of one event.

During a deepening, make sure that your patient knows that nothing will harm him. You do not want your client to imagine tripping down a set of stairs. Say things like, "With each step you take, you are going deeper and deeper into a very, very, deep state of relaxation. You feel comfortable and safe."

And, as in the above example, always tie in the fact that the client is going "deeper." Make sure that you communicate that with each step (or floor, if you are sending a client down an escalator) your client goes down, he is going deeper into his subconscious. Do not just tell him to go down the stairs, tell him that those stairs are allowing him to go deeper as you count the steps. "Ten, take the first step down. Nine, another step deeper."

By the time the client is at the bottom of the stairs, he will be relaxed and slowed down.

If your client is on an escalator, before the counting begins, tell your client that it is a long escalator and that by the time you get to one, he will be at the bottom. Otherwise, your client may imagine himself at the bottom of the escalator when you are at the count of five. Make sure that you spell out everything for him.

You may want to say, "Ten, moving down a little bit. Nine, moving deeper a little more, down the escalator. With each floor you go down, you are so much more relaxed. You are ten times more relaxed every foot you move down, down, down."

As with an induction, feel free to incorporate activities that the client likes into the deepening. If you have an adventurous client who relaxes by repelling (an activity that causes the rest of us to feel sheer terror!), use a deepening that involves repelling the client down a mountain. However, make sure that the client feels safe. Tell him that the ropes are secure and that nothing bad is going to happen.

No matter what scenario you use, be sure to tell your client that nothing bad will happen. The client will not fall down the stairs and will not run into a tree while skiing down the hill; the elevator will not get stuck.

Because hypnotherapy is positive, I like to use positive phrasing wherever possible. Do not say, "In this particular trip down the side of the hill, you will not run into a tree." Although you are telling the client he will not run into a tree, this phrase will be planted in his mind and he may envision it nonetheless. Say something like, "In this particular trip down the side of a hill, nothing will happen to you. It will be smooth. It will be your smoothest trip down the side of a hill ever."

Do not let the client's imagination run wild.

Be sure to coordinate a downward motion with downward counting, and the client going downward into hypnosis.

Remember to use words such as "deeper," "down," and "relaxing." These words imply deepness and slowing down.

Also, frequently use and stretch out the word "and." For example, "You are relaxing more deeply, annnnnnnd unwinding completely." Clients report finding this quite relaxing. It also helps to tie your instructions together in a relaxing way.

By using all of these tricks of the trade, your session will be successful.

Many of my patients say that in addition to the problem for which they came to see me, they cannot relax. These same patients often leave feeling more relaxed than they thought possible, and much of this is due to the deepening. Like having a massage, a hypnotherapy session is a perfect opportunity for the client to relax. In fact, many people compare hypnotherapy to massage in the sense that it offers relaxation. Unlike massage therapists, hypnotherapists add positive suggestions for change, but the type of relaxation is very similar.

Though there are clients who might drop immediately into Theta or Delta during the induction, do not omit the deepening in the first session. In subsequent visits, feel free to skip the deepening if the client falls into Theta or Delta immediately, but *do not omit the deepening during the first visit.*

Aside from physical indicators such as slowed breathing or slowed pulse (observed visually on the neck, head, and hands), you also can roughly ascertain what state of consciousness a client goes into by having a discussion with him at the conclusion of the session. If the client's last memory of the first session occurred about two minutes into the induction, and he appears to be equally relaxed during subsequent inductions, you can safely skip the deepening. This client obviously goes into a deep trance quickly. If you are unsure, use the deepening. It will not hurt.

Sample Deepening 1

You are completely relaxed and contented as you stand at the edge of the lake, and hear the rocking of a small rowboat as it floats gently next to a small dock. The dock is inviting, and you hear the call of baby ducks as they swim circles around their mother, safely and securely, near the end of the dock.

The well-constructed wooden dock has ten evenly spaced planks for steps, and handrails that lead to a wide platform, to which the small white rowboat is tied. There is an antique iron park bench sitting at the end of the dock, overlooking the lake. There are tiny peeping noises coming from the ducklings. You will go down the steps, one by one, confidently. And you will count them backwards from 10 to 1. And as you count them, you will go deeper and deeper into your trance with each and every step you descend

You know that you are safe and secure as you grab hold of the sturdy handrails and move calmly to the top step. Ten. And you are going deeper and deeper. You feel comfortable and relaxed as you step onto the next step. Nine.

You can feel the smooth, wooden handrail as you slide your hands along it and go down another step and go deeper, and deeper. Eight. The planks are warm from the sun and inviting on your feet as you go down another step. Seven. You slide your hands a little further down the handrail and step down again, going deeper and deeper. Six. You see the baby ducks swim into the cool shadows of the dock as you take another step down.

The bump, bump, bump of the rowboat continues as you go down another step, and you are relaxed and contented. Five. Stepping further down, the mother duck calls her babies, and you are going deeper. Four. The rhythmic waves lap onto the shore, and you lower yourself onto the next plank. Three. You are more relaxed, as you calmly go down another step. Two. The ducklings come out from under the dock, to join their mother, as you take the step safely onto the platform. One.

Note: Reading time of this deepening is approximately 3 minutes and 30 seconds. The author did not indicate any (pauses), which may be added, if desired, to allow the client to go deeper on his own. Pauses would extend the time needed to complete the deepening.

Sample Deepening 2

Take a step down now ... down to the ninth step. Smoothly and easily. Feel yourself going deeper. Now down to step eight ... going deeper still.

Now down to step seven ... going deeper ... down to step six ... deeper still ... going further down to step five ... and step four ... step three ... two ... one. Now you are standing on the floor below. There is a door in front of you. A sign on the door reads "Doorway to the Beach of Relaxation." Reach out and turn the doorknob. Open the door. A stream of golden sunlight pours through the open door. Walk through the door into the golden sunlight.

Before you, stretches a beach of pure white sand. Beyond the edge of the beach is an endless ocean of clear blue water. Walk on the beach until you come to the place where the dry sand meets the wet sand, near the water's edge. Stand here a moment and notice all of the sights and sounds.

Notice the seagulls in the sky above. Watch them diving for fish in the sea below. Listen to their chatter as they return to the sky. Notice the other birds around you. They show their appreciation for life in their smooth flight and the happy songs they sing.

Notice the majestic expanse of the ocean in front of you. A gentle wave comes ashore and rushes past your feet. Feel how it pleasantly glides past your feet as it recedes back into the ocean. This ocean is the "sea of relaxation." With each wave that touches the sand, you are feeling more and more deeply relaxed.

Helpful Tip

If you have several clients in one day, you may find yourself beginning to get sleepy, especially during the deepenings. To combat fatigue, you may want to create a hypnotherapy recording for yourself, which programs you to maintain full awakening consciousness and mental sharpness during your sessions.

Suggested Practice

Write a 10-unit deepening. Incorporate counting from 10 down to one, making sure that the client knows he will be going deeper as the numbers decrease. Record the process.

When you are done with this, you should have a recording with an induction, 30 to 60 seconds of silence, a deepening (three to five minutes in length), and another 30 to 60 seconds of silence. (Obviously, you do not need to record this final silence. I mention it so that you will remember to include it when you add the next part, the script, which is discussed in my books, Hypnotherapy Scripts Volumes I & II, which are now available at http://www.stevegjones.com/books.htm.)

Test Your Knowledge on Chapter 2 - Deepenings
(See back of book for correct answers)

- **Question 1**

In a deepening, you are correlating downward motion (e.g. going down some stairs), downward counting (10 to 1), and what else?

- **Question 2**

Where on the client's body can you look for signs of their bodily processes slowing down?

- **Question 3**

How many sets of deepenings should be used in one hypnotherapy session?

- **Question 4**

If you are unsure of a client's "deepness," should you omit the deepening?

Chapter 3

Collection of Inductions and Deepenings

The following is a collection of hypnotherapy inductions and deepenings using many different scenarios. Feel free to use them on yourself, friends, and clients. Also, feel free to make any appropriate changes to suit your particular needs.

Beach 1 Induction

Alright now. Close your eyes. Focus on relaxing your body and putting your mind at ease. Take a deep breath. Filling your lungs with air...very slowly. Very good. Now open your mouth just a little bit and slowly let the air out of your lungs. You feel yourself relax. Now again, inhale deeply, expanding your chest very slowly. Hold it here. And slowly breathe out, relaxing even more with every second you push the air out. You focus on becoming completely at ease. Once again, inhale slowly, feeling your body rise. And hold it for just one second, and slowly release, feeling your chest go back down. Your breathing is consistent and relaxes you. Now focus on your breathing. [pause] Now you are going to go to a place that helps you relax even more. You will be more relaxed than you ever have before. You are on a beach. As you stand on the beach, your senses come alive and you notice every detail around you. You look at the white sandy beach to your left and right, it seems to go on forever in both directions. You look out at the water. There are little waves coming toward you. Look at the color of the water; it is brilliant blue. You see water as far as your eyes can see. You look up at the sky and you notice sea gulls flying above. You can hear their calls to each other. Notice how they glide in the air, so effortlessly. You walk closer to the water. You are on the waters edge. Feel the water surround your feet and ankles. The water is warm and refreshing. You wiggle your toes in the sand; it feels good on your bare feet. You take a little while to listen to the soft sounds of the waves breaking on the shore. Every wave you see rolling in toward you, relaxes you even more. You take a deep breath in and smell the salty air. It smells clean and pure. You are completely at ease. You decide to take a little walk down the beach. You walk very slowly, enjoying every step that you take. You are at complete peace here on the beach. You continue to walk. There is no one on this beach except you. You feel very comfortable here. As you walk, you bend down and pick up a shell. It's light pink and white. You run your fingers around it and it's smooth on one side and bumpy on the outside. You put it to your ear and you can hear the sound of the ocean. You put the shell back on the beach and you continue your walk. You come to a large comfortable blanket and you decide to lay down on it. You are on your back and you feel the warm breeze sweeping across your body. Your body is cushioned by the sand and the blanket. You relax your entire body. Focus on your head. Ease the muscles in your temples. That's right, your head feels good. Now open your mouth just a little and relax your jaw. Let all tension disappear. Roll your neck to both sides and let all the muscles in your neck and upper body relax. Work your way down through your arms. Let your shoulders, arms and hands go limp by your side. Focus on your lower back and stomach area. Feel as each inch relaxes. You feel good. Your upper body is at ease. Now focus down to your hips and buttocks; all tension is released. Go further now. To your thighs; let them relax and go limp. You are very relaxed on the blanket surrounded by sand. Now focus further down on your body to your knees, calves, and shins. Bend your knees slightly and let them relax. You move your ankles slightly so that there is no tension in them. That's right, feel all tension leave your legs. That feels good. Relax the arch of your foot and wiggle your toes. Your entire body now is relaxed. You are now more relaxed than you have ever felt before. You lay on the blanket, your body completely at ease. You feel the warm air rush over you. You can hear the waves nearby. It feels so good to completely unwind. You enjoy the feeling of getting rid of all tension in your body and mind. Now, you lay there on the blanket very still and you continue to relax.

Beach 1 Deepening

You now slowly sit up and open your eyes and look out to the beautiful water and sky. You notice the sun and all the colors on the horizon. The sky is filled with shades of red, orange, pink, and purple. You see that the sun is close to setting. As I count from 10, the sun sets closer to the horizon and you relax deeper and deeper with every number I count. Okay...Ten...the sun goes down just a little and you feel yourself relax. Nine...you are going deeper into relaxation. You see the sun lower and you are feeling very good. Eight...deeper still...Seven...You are feeling more and more relaxed as you watch the sun go down. Six...you relax further into hypnosis...Five...the sun is another step closer to setting on the horizon and you are very relaxed...Four...You relax deeper...Three...
Deeper still. You watch the sun go down...down. Two...you are very relaxed and at the count of the next number you will be completely relaxed...One. You are very relaxed. Very comfortable. We will now focus on your subconscious mind to make changes and go forward.

Beach 2 (private island) Induction

Okay now, close your eyes. Let your entire body loosen. Now take three deep breaths on my call. Okay...Breath in...expand your lungs, filling them with air. That's good. Hold it here for a second...and slowly press it out. Get all of the air out of your lungs. Good, you are feeling more relaxed now. Alright now, breathe in again. Air coming through your nose, feel your chest rise. That's it, really fill up those lungs. Now hold. Open your mouth just a little bit, relax your jaw...and...let out all the air. Slowly release. Feel your chest deflate back down. You are even more relaxed now. Okay, one more time, breathe in slowly. Allow yourself time to fill your lungs. That's good...now hold your breath...and release through your mouth. You are now very relaxed. Not only is your body at ease, but so is your mind. Now, lets take a journey. This journey will involve your five senses and will further relax you. You find yourself on your own private island. You are on the beach. You notice that the island is small, seeing that the beach curves in either direction, surrounding a jungle. Look out at the water. Notice the colors of the water. Picture the clear water. Notice the reef just beyond the sand causes the water to have seven shades of blue and green. You see turquoise, light green, brilliant blue, sea foam green, and several other colors. You look up at the sky and notice how bright blue it is. There are several large clouds in the sky. They are big and white. You notice them move slowly in the sky and change shapes. Watch the clouds as they transform in front of you. [pause] The water then distracts you. You notice about 100 yards in front of you there is a barrier in the water. This barrier is protecting your island and causing the waves to break on it. Listen to the waves hit and break on the rocks. The sound is soothing and you enjoy it. You take a few steps forward and walk into the water. It is completely calm here. The water is warm. Feel it against your legs. The water is soothing to your skin; this relaxes you and puts your mind at ease. You decide to get out of the water. You walk slowly across the beach and into the grove of palm trees. As you walk, a coconut falls from a palm tree just in front of you. You decide to take this coconut and hit it across a rock. This opens the coconut and at first you smell the coconut. It smells sweet and calms you. You then tilt the coconut and taste the coconut milk. It tastes clean and sweet. You leave the coconut behind and continue walking through the palm trees. As you walk, you admire the tall palms swaying in the breeze. You then look in front of you and notice there is a small clearing of trees. In between two trees is a hammock. You decide to lay in this hammock and rest. You climb in and get very comfortable. The hammock sways very gently. As you lay here, you focus on relaxing your entire body. You start with your head. Relax the muscles in your face and in your jaw. That's good. Moving down to your neck and shoulders, you relax every muscle. Feel all tension release. Your arms, hands, and fingers lay loosely by your side as you sway on the hammock. Focus on relaxing your core, your lower back, sides, and abs. Now moving further down your body, to your hips and buttocks, you relax these muscles even more. That feels good doesn't it? Relax your thighs. Relax your knees. Relax your calves and shins. Your legs are now completely lifeless. Move down to your ankles, feet, and toes. There is no tension in your feet. Your entire body is now very relaxed. Enjoy this relaxation. Now focus on relaxing your mind. You do not cloud your brain with random thoughts. You focus on relaxing further and enjoying swaying in the hammock. You enjoy this feeling of total relaxation of your body and mind.

Beach 2 (private island) Deepening (walking down a dune)

You easily and effortlessly get out of the hammock and walk a little farther into the jungle of palm trees. All of a sudden, there are no more trees and you are looking out at the ocean on top of a large sand dune. In this sand dune, there is a pathway of 10 steps leading down onto the sandy beach. You stand on top of this dune and look down the steps. I will now count down from ten. You will step down each time and as you do so, you will become even more relaxed. You will become more deeply relaxed with every step down that you take. 10 you are at the top now, feeling relaxed...9...you take a step down and as you do you are more at ease...8...deeper now...7...more deeply relaxed with each step...6...that's good. You are feeling very relaxed. 5...down, down, more relaxed...4...3...you are feeling extremely relaxed now...2 and on the count of the next number you will be completely relaxed...1. You are in a complete state of relaxation. You are now more relaxed than you ever have before. Now we will focus on _____ and you will be ready to make positive changes in your life.

Beach 3 Induction (pier)

Okay, you are going to take five deep breaths. Each deep breath is going to relax you. Alright now, breath in deeply and slowly, focusing on the consistent rise of your chest. That's good. Now hold it for one second...and...slowly let it out. Don't push it, just easily and effortlessly let it out. You are feeling more relaxed now. Now again, breathe in. Fill your lungs to capacity. Excellent and hold. Now release, feeling your shoulders go down...three more times. And...breathe in, deep breath...hold here...and let it all out...very good. Now again, take a deep breath, slowly expanding your lungs...until you can't fill them any more...and...release the air, slowly, that feels good. Okay, once more...breathe in slowly feeling your chest rise...that's good, hold here...and release, letting all that air out. Feel yourself relax. You feel loose and light, it's a great feeling being relaxed. Now I am going to describe a place to you. You will picture yourself here. It will be very relaxing and you will enjoy being there. Now, picture yourself on a long wooden pier that goes over a beach and extends out to the ocean. You walk along this pier, barefoot, holding your shoes. The warm, smooth wood feels good on your bare feet. You walk slowly taking in your surroundings. You notice an old man fishing over the side of the pier; he is enjoying himself just like you are. You continue walking. You take a deep breath in. The warm air fills your lungs and you feel refreshed. You smell the slight scent of ocean and the smell refreshes you too. It smells clean and natural. As you walk, you pass by two children playing and looking over the pier. They do not disturb you as you continue to walk along the pier. You are enjoying this walk. You find it so easy to relax. You enjoy looking out into the never-ending blue sky. Occasionally you see pelicans gliding across the water in the distance. You see large fluffy clouds moving very slowly across the sky. You are really enjoying yourself. You now come to the end of the pier. At the end of the long planks of wood, there is a comfortable bench with cushions on it. You decide to sit and relax further. As you sit, you get comfortable and you close your eyes. You can feel the breeze gradually warming your body. You feel very good and relaxed. Your mind is at ease and you focus on relaxing every inch of your body. You start with your head. You relax your forehead, then your mouth, and your jaw. You sit there for a second and allow your head to be more relaxed than it ever has before. You relax your neck and shoulders. Allow your head to rest easily on top. Let your arms, hands, and finger hang loosely by your side. That's right, you are feeling very good. You move down your back and torso, letting each muscle loosen. You allow your waist, hips and buttocks to relax. As you continue to relax your upper body, you feel another slight gust of warm air sweep around your body; it feels nice. You continue on relaxing and focusing on your body. Now feel your thighs begin to relax, they become so relaxed that you can't tell that you are sitting on them. Move down to your knees, they are supported by the bench and your thighs, but they too relax. You now relax your calves, shins, and all the muscles in your ankles. It feels good to no longer walk on your feet. You give your feet and toes a break and relax each toe, one by one. You enjoy feeling this way. You like taking time for yourself. You are improving your body and soul by relaxing them. You continue sitting in your comfortable bench. You reflect only on how good you feel and how relaxed you are. All thoughts and memories do not occur to you at this point in time. Now continue to sit and relax.

Beach 3 Deepening

Now picture yourself at the other end of the pier on top of a staircase that leads you down to the beach. It's a staircase with 10 steps. There is a sturdy railing to either side. The steps are sturdy too. I am going to count down from ten and as I count, you will take a step down. With each step that you take, you will become more and more relaxed. Ten...take the first step down. That's right, feel yourself relax. Nine, take another step...relaxing further. Eight...becoming more and more hypnotized. Seven...becoming even more relaxed with each step...feeling good. Six...deeper and deeper as you go down. Five...another step down...feeling more relaxed. Four...down a step...deeply into a relaxed state and three...further down...down. Two...and on the count of the next number you will be completely relaxed. One. You are completely relaxed and feeling good.

Beach 4 Induction

Okay, go ahead and get comfortable. Feel free to move around a little or scratch an itch. Now, close your eyes. You are going to take three deep breaths on my call, in order to relax you. Alright...in through your nose...hold...and out through your mouth. Very good. And in again, filling your lungs with air...slowly breathing in...and...release slowly...that's good. One last deep breath...breathe in filling your lungs and feeling your chest rise...hold here for a second...and slowly let it all out...take your time. Excellent. You should be feeling a little more relaxed. Okay, now you are going to go to a very relaxing and peaceful place. You are at the beach. There are a few other people on the beach, but they do not disturb you or notice you. You walk along the beach, taking a leisurely stroll. It's a beautiful day. The clouds move along, sometimes blocking the sun and sometimes letting the suns rays pour through. The sun is bright and it warms your body and soul. You feel very peaceful and at ease. You bend down and scoop up a handful of sand. The sand is white and very fine. It feels like a mixture of flour and sugar. You rub it between your thumb and fingers and you let fall back to the beach. You stand there, staring at the water and the sky. It's such a beautiful sight. The color of the water reflects perfectly with the sky. You take a deep breath in, filling your lungs with the air. The air smells a little salty. You enjoy the smell of the beach. The salty smell calms you and relaxes you. As you look up at the sky, down one side of the beach, you notice several kites flying in the wind. Some kites are steady and stay in one place. Other kites more erratically, dive bombing toward the beach and the ocean. The kites have brilliant colors... bright pink, green, and yellow. They stand out perfectly against the blue of the sky. You turn in the opposite direction and start walking down to the other end of the beach. You notice some sand crabs scurrying across the beach as you walk by them. The sand feels very good against your feet. The sand is soft and warm. You continue walking, enjoying yourself and relaxing. Your mind and body are at ease. You have no stresses or worries. You take in your surroundings. You appreciate nature and you enjoy all that Mother Nature has to offer. As you continue to walk, you come across a sandcastle. The sandcastle is very large and ornate. In the center of it is a flag pole with a flag flapping in the breeze. The castle is designed like a fort, shaped like a square with the pole in the middle. Outside of the castle is a moat to collect water. This castle has all sorts of towers on each corner. It obviously took someone a long time to put this sandcastle together. You decide to put a towel down on the beach and lie down and relax. As you lay there with your eyes closed, you can hear the waves breaking on the shore. The sound is consistent and very relaxing. You lay there and as you do, you focus on relaxing every inch of your body. Focus on your head. Relax the muscles in your temples. That's right, your head feels good and at ease. You open your mouth just a little and let your jaw hang. Let all tension disappear. You roll your neck and let all the muscles in your neck and upper body relax. Work your way down to your arms. Let your shoulders, arms and hands go limp by your side. Focus on your lower back and stomach area. Feel as each inch relaxes. You feel good. Your upper body is at ease. Now focus down to your hips and buttocks; all tension is released. Go further now. To your thighs; let them relax and go limp. You are very relaxed on the towel surrounded by sand. Now focus further down on your body to your knees, calves, and shins. Bend your knees slightly and let them relax. You move your ankles slightly so that there is no tension in them. That's right, feel all tension leave your legs. That feels good. Relax the arch of your foot and wiggle your toes. Your entire body now is relaxed. You are now more relaxed than you have ever felt before. You lay on the blanket, your body completely at ease. You feel the warm air rush over you. You can hear the waves nearby. It feels so good to completely unwind. You enjoy the feeling of getting rid of all tension in your body and mind. Now, you lay there on the blanket very still and you continue to relax.

Steve G. Jones, M.Ed.

Beach 4 Deepening

You now slowly sit up and open your eyes and look out to the beautiful water and sky. You notice the flag on the pole sticking up 10 feet from the sand castle. There is a man that appears to be lowering the flag. As I count from 10, the flag lowers and you relax deeper and deeper with every number I count. Okay...Ten...the flag goes down just a little and you feel yourself relax. Nine...you are going deeper into relaxation. You see the flag lower and you are feeling very good. Eight...deeper still...Seven...You are feeling more and more relaxed as you watch the flag lower. Six...you relax further into hypnosis...Five...the flag is now lower and you are very relaxed...Four...You relax deeper...Three...deeper still. You watch the flag go down...down. Two...you are very relaxed and at the count of the next number you will be completely relaxed...One. You are very relaxed. Very comfortable. We will now focus on your subconscious mind to make changes and go forward.

Beach 5 Induction (resort)

Okay. You are laying down on a very comfortable sofa. Go ahead and close your eyes. You feel good and very comfortable. Lets pause as you clear your mind of any thoughts. [pause] Okay, that's good. Now you are going to take 3 deep breaths. Breathe in, filling your lungs until they are full. Verrry slowly. That's good. And now…release the air, letting it out through your mouth. You should feel a little more relaxed. Okay, once again, take a big deep breath. Really fill up your lungs. Feel your chest rise. And hold for a second…and let it all out slowly. Excellent. Okay, one more deep breath. In through the nose, filling your lungs…now open your mouth and relax your jaw…and release, slowly and barely pushing the air out. Very good. You should be feeling a little more relaxed now. Now, picture yourself at a resort. It's a five star resort where the staff caters to your every need. You are sitting on a lounger that is made of beautiful dark wood and on top is a very comfortable cushion. You have the lounger tilted halfway back so that you are laying down, but you still have a beautiful view of the water. Next to you is a little side table where your pina colada is sitting. You pick it up and take a sip. It tastes and smells sweet like coconut and pineapple. There is a pretty red umbrella sticking out at the top of the drink. You put your drink back down and admire the view. The water is perfectly clear and you can see a reef under the water just a hundred yards out. The reef makes the water have seven different shades of blue and green. It is a beautiful sight, of which you have never seen before. Just past the reef, you see a small sailboat with a passenger or two. They are moving very slowly from your left, to your right. The sail is very pretty. It has colors of bright pink and yellow. The colors really stand out against the blue of the water. As you look out to the water, you notice that past the sail boat is a speed boat with a parasail behind it. There is someone way up in the air. You are glad you are sitting on the beach, relaxing and taking time for yourself. You enjoy this time alone. You are very peaceful. You notice that the sun is high in the sky and you grab your suntan lotion and start applying it to your body. Your skin feels warm and smooth. You put the lotion all over your body and sit back in your chair. There aren't many people on the beach. You like to imagine that you are the only one there. You don't hear any people talking, all you hear is the sound of the small waves coming in and occasionally you hear the call of a bird. The sound of the bird does not bother you, the sound is unfamiliar to you, but it reminds you that you are in a beautiful tropical paradise. You decide to put your chair all the way back and close your eyes. You feel so calm on this beach. You focus on relaxing your entire body. You let your head rest on the back of the lounger. You relax your neck and shoulders. You arms and hands hang loosely by the sides of your body. You let your back arch just slightly and then you relax each vertebra one at a time down to the base of your spine. You relax your chest, stomach, and hips. You wiggle your hips and buttocks back and forth, making sure they are very comfortable. You let your legs open just a little, relaxing your thighs and knees. You let your ankles and feet part a little too. You elongate your legs, feet, and toes. Every inch of you is now relaxed. You haven't felt this good in a long time. You enjoy yourself as you lay still, your body completely relaxed. You feel the warm rays of the sun penetrate your body. You feel the cool breeze sweep over your body. You hear the soothing sound of the water splashing against the beach. Your mind and are in very relaxed state. You continue to relax...

Beach 5 Deepening

You now slowly sit up on your lounger and open your eyes and look out to the beautiful water and sky. You notice a kite being flown far out into the sky. As I count down from 10, the kite lowers and you relax deeper and deeper with every number I count. Okay...Ten...the kite moves slowly down just a little and you feel yourself relax. Nine...you are going deeper into a state of relaxation. You see the kite lower and you are feeling very good. Eight...deeper still...Seven...You are feeling more and more relaxed as you watch the kite lower. Six...you relax further into hypnosis...Five...the kite is now lower and you are very relaxed...Four...You relax deeper...Three...Deeper still. You watch the kite go down...down. Two...you are very relaxed and at the count of the next number you will be completely relaxed...One. You are very relaxed. Very comfortable. We will now focus on your subconscious mind to make positive changes and go forward with your life.

City 1 Induction (shopping)

Alright now. Close your eyes. Focus on relaxing your body and putting your mind at ease. Take a deep breath...filling your lungs with air...very slowly...very good...now open your mouth just a little bit and...exhale...slowly let the air out of your lungs. You feel yourself relax. Now again...inhale deeply...expanding your chest very slowly...hold it here...and slowly breathe out...relaxing even more with every second you push the air out. You focus on becoming completely at ease. Last deep breath...inhale slowly...feeling your chest rise...and hold...and slowly release...feeling your chest go back down. Your breathing is consistent and relaxes you. Now focus on your breathing. [pause] Now you are going to go to a place that helps you relax even more. You will be more relaxed than you ever have before. Picture yourself in a bustling city. You are riding on the subway. There are all sorts of different people around you. You are sure that each one has an interesting story to tell. The subway comes to a halt and it reaches your destination. You take step onto the platform and move to the side so that others can get onto the subway. You turn around and watch as the doors close and the train accelerates through the tunnel. In only seconds it is gone. You turn around and walk up the large cement steps. As you walk up, it gets brighter and brighter. When you reach the top, you see people walking on the sidewalks in every direction. You jump right in and blend into the crowd. As you walk down the street, you are aware of all the different sounds. In a big city like this, there are many sounds for you to listen to. You hear the engines of cars, buses, and motorcycles and along with the rumbling sound of engines, is the beeping of horns. You don't mind this sound, you are happy and content whenever you walking along the streets. You hear the sounds of people chatting around you. Some are talking with companions, others are talking on there cell phones. You continue to enjoy yourself in the crowd. You take a look at the buildings around you. They are tall and tower high above you. You can see very little of the sky, but you can tell that it is a brilliant blue and a wonderful day to go shopping. You look at the different storefronts as you walk along. You pass stores that have furniture in display cases. You pass restaurants, bakeries, and butchers. You come to an area of the street that is mainly clothing shopping. You decide to go into one of the stores because it has beautiful clothes on display on the mannequins in front. You walk in, and the store instantly puts you at ease. A nice lady greets you and lets you know that she is there to help. You begin looking admirably at the clothes. There are all sorts of different clothes made from different fabrics. Your eye is caught by a beautiful silk dress. You hold the soft fabric between your fingertips. It feels smooth and slippery. You imagine what the fabric would feel like against your skin. You walk out of the store and continue to go in and out of different stores, trying things on and buying a few items. You enjoy shopping. It relaxes you and gives you time to spend to yourself. You like looking at all the clothes and seeing what is in style. You continue to walk on the sidewalk, blending in with the people around you. You take a deep breath in and as you do, you notice the smell of food. There are several vendors selling food to passersby. You take in all the different smells of food and continue on your way. As you walk, you find your body relaxing. You walk with your head held high and relaxed. Your shoulders are square with no tension. Your back is straight and at ease. Your arms dangle by your side carrying a few bags. You enjoy your walk through the city and you become more relaxed as you walk. Your legs loosen. You stretch them out with each step that you take. The shoes that you are wearing are comfortable, yet stylish. Your feet and toes feel as if they are walking on clouds. You continue to enjoy your walk along the streets of the city. You admire the stores and they tall buildings around you. You continue to relax as you walk along.

Steve G. Jones, M.Ed.

City 1 Deepening

You are standing on the top of a large cement staircase, leading down toward the subway. You take a look and notice that there are ten steps to the train platform. As I count from ten, you are going take a step down. As you take a step down, you are going to become more and more relaxed. When you reach the bottom, you will be more relaxed than you have ever felt before. Ten...you take a step down...easily...and effortlessly...Nine...you are feeling more relaxed...Eight...down...down you go...down the stairs...Seven...deeper into a state of deep relaxation...Six...deeper still...Five...feeling more and more relaxed...Four...down another step...down you go...feeling very good...Three...more and more deeply relaxed...Two...and on the count of the next number...you will be more relaxed than you ever have been before...One...you are in a deep state of relaxation. You are now more relaxed than you ever have been before. You continue to relax. Your body and mind are at peace and you are ready to make positive changes to your life.

City 2 Induction (people watching)

Go ahead and get comfortable in the chair you are laying on and close your eyes. You are going to take five deep breaths. Each deep breath is going to relax you. Alright now...inhale...focusing on the consistent rise of your chest...hold...and...slowly let it out...just easily and effortlessly let it out. You are feeling more relaxed now. Now again, breathe in...filling your lungs...excellent and hold...now release, feeling your shoulders go down. Three more times. And...breathe in, deep breath...hold here...and let it all out...very good. Now again...inhale...slowly expanding your lungs ...and...release the air...slowly...relaxing as you do so. Okay...once more...inhale deeply...hold here...and release...letting all that air out. Feel yourself relax. Picture yourself on a balcony in a large city. This balcony overlooks a beautiful park. You are standing out on this balcony people watching. You lean against the railing on the balcony and you run your hand along it. You see that it is very strong and sturdy. There is a street below you with sidewalks on either side. There are a lot of cars in the street. Most of them are taxis. You can see yellow car after yellow car below. Some have their lights on top of the roof on and some don't. There are a lot of people walking on the sidewalks below. You see a business man in a suit with a briefcase in hand. You see a woman dressed for work also talking on a cell phone. You see a mom walking two small children to school. You see students with backpacks on possibly walking to class. Since you are right next to the park, you also notice many people with their dogs walking into the park. You see two dog owners cross paths on the street below and you hear the dogs barking at each other as the people continue quickly down the street. You hear other dogs joyfully barking in the park. You enjoy seeing people take time out of their day to walk their dogs. It's a very nice day outside. The sky is blue and the sun is shining. You go back to watching people on the street. You wonder where some of the people are going. You imagine some of them are going grocery shopping and running errands. Perhaps some are on their way to meet other people. You see some people with bags in their hands, perhaps spending the day shopping. You see people with cameras, taking pictures. You wonder if maybe they are tourists. You enjoy trying to figure out where people are going. Just as you think you have figured it out, another person comes along that you try to figure out. You take a deep breath in and you smell the scent of hot dogs from a vendor below. You look at people as they stop to get lunch at the hot dog stand. Your attention turns back to the park. It is autumn and the trees in the park are turning brilliant shades of red, orange, and yellow. You see a group of people in a field, playing Frisbee. You watch as the Frisbee is thrown from someone's hand and glides low to the ground into another person's hand. You watch for a little while as the Frisbee goes back and forth. This motion relaxes you. You decide to sit down on a lounge chair on the balcony. This chair has plush cushions for you to sit on. You put your head back and prop your feet up and close your eyes. All sounds and smells fade away. You focus on relaxing your entire body. You allow all muscles from the top of your head…all the way down to your toes…you allow all the muscles to loosen and relax. One…muscle…at…a…time. You clear your mind of any thoughts. You enjoy the suns warm rays as your body soaks them up on this cool autumn day. There is a slight breeze that sweeps across your body, further relaxing you. You let your head relax on the cushion. You allow your entire body to sink into the chair. Your arms rest by your side and your legs and feet loosen as you lay there enjoying time to yourself. You continue to relax…

City 2 Deepening

You are standing in a hallway on the tenth floor waiting for an elevator. The car arrives and the doors open. You walk inside the elevator and the doors close. You press the button that takes to the ground level. You watch the number of the floor descend, starting with floor number ten. As you watch the numbers go down, you will feel yourself relax with each floor. Ten...the elevator starts moving to take you down...Nine...you relax as you watch the numbers drop...Eight...down...down the elevator goes...Seven...you relax deeper with ever floor you pass...Six...deeper   still...Five...down...down   you go...Four...relaxing more and more deeply into a deep state of relaxation...Three...down further...relaxing as you go...Two...and on the count of the next number...you will be   more   relaxed   than   you   have   ever   been before...One...relaxed now...you are in a deep state of relaxation. Your mind and body are at ease and you are now ready to make positive changes in your life.

City 3 Induction (sight seeing)

You are lying down in a very comfortable chair. Go ahead and close your eyes. Lets pause as you clear your mind of any thoughts. [pause] Now take 3 deep breaths. Inhale deeply...filling your lungs to capacity...very slowly...and now...release the air...letting it out through your mouth. You should feel a little more relaxed. Another deep breath, inhale...take a big deep breath. Feel your shoulders rise. And hold for a second...and let it all out slowly...exhale. Excellent. One more deep breath. In through the nose...inhaling...filling your lungs...now open your mouth and relax your jaw...and release...exhale...slowly and barely pushing the air out. Very good. You should be feeling more relaxed now. Now picture yourself in New York City. You are exploring the island of Manhattan and sightseeing. You enjoy taking in all the sights. You start your journey in Central Park. There are lots of people having picnics in the grass and walking their dogs. It's a pretty summer day. Flowers all over the park are in bloom. The trees are leafy, green, and lush with the rain the city got a few days ago. You continue your walk. You leave central park and you join the people walking on the streets. It's a nice day out today. You look up at the tall buildings. They are so tall, you can't see the top of them. You realize you are near the empire state building, and you decide to go to the top. You enjoy the elevators as they zip to the top of the building. When you reach the top, you look out at the city. There are buildings all around you. They all vary in size and structure. There are old ones made of stone and there are newer ones made of glass. You can see the boroughs surrounding the city. You look out at the rivers and bay and the sun is glistening off the water. The city is small, but so densely packed. You know that's what makes it so great. You are able to see everything you want to see in one day. You lean up against the fencing at the top of the Empire State building. You rest your fingers on the fence and peer out. It's a very relaxing sight. There are no sounds up here, only the sounds of people talking as they pass by you. The air is fresh up here and smells very clean. You decide to go back down the building and continue exploring the city. You enjoy walking. It relaxes you and you enjoy the exercise. You continue on to Times Square. There are people milling all about. You hear the sounds of people talking, horns beeping, and cars driving. It's quite a contrast to the top of the Empire State Building. Times Square is filled with flashing lights and lots of color even in the daytime. You see advertisements everywhere and the big Virgin sign. You enjoy walking along the sidewalk, taking in the sights. You decide to get on the subway to the lower end of the city. The subway gets you there much faster than if you had walked. You decide to get out in Chinatown and explore. You get off the subway, step onto the platform and climb the stairs onto the street. You now feel like you have entered another country. There is Chinese writing all around. You see the color red everywhere, but you see a lot of other colors too. You take a deep breath in and you can smell the tasty Chinese food. It smells very good and gets your stomach churning. You pass by a shop that sells colorful paper lanterns. You admire them for a second and continue to walk. You walk through the financial distract. You admire the tall buildings all around you. And you end your walk in Battery Park. The park is very calm and peaceful. You are now away from the hustle and bustle of city life. You walk along the sidewalk near the waters edge. You watch as the ferry transports people over to the statue of liberty. You watch the ferry as it slowly drifts away from you and closer to the small island in the middle of the harbor. The statue of liberty stands strong and you admire her. You decide to sit down on a bench and sit back and relax. It feels good to rest your body after your day of sightseeing. Slowly, your entire body starts to calm down. Your head rests easily on your neck and shoulders. Each muscle and every vertebra in your back loosens and relaxes. You let your arms hang loosely by your sides. You stretch out your legs in front of you and allow them to relax. You roll your ankles around and point and flex your feet until they feel loose and at ease. You close your eyes and continue to relax as you think back to your day.

Steve G. Jones, M.Ed.

City 3 Deepening

You go back to earlier in your day and you are in the elevator at the Empire State Building. You are going to hear me count down from ten. As I count down from ten, the elevator is going to bring you down to the lobby. As the elevator takes you down, you are going to relax deeper and deeper with every floor. Ten...down the elevator goes...Nine...you relax as you go down...down toward the lobby...Eight...you are becoming more deeply relaxed...Seven...deeper still...Six...down...down you go in the elevator...Five...feel yourself at peace as you relax more and more...Four...you enjoy the movement of the elevator...as you go down...down...Three...you relaxing more and more...Two...and at the count of the next number...the elevator doors are going to open and you are going to be in a complete state of relaxation...One...doors open...you are now completely relaxed. You are now more relaxed than you have ever been before. You enjoy this sensation sweeping across your body. You are at ease and at peace with yourself. You are ready to make positive changes to your life.

Driving Car 1 Induction (winding road in California)

As you sit in your comfortable chair, go ahead and close your eyes. Now in order to relax, take three deep breaths. In through your nose...deeply...and...slowly...that's good. Hold here...and let it all out through your mouth. Very good. Another breath in...very slowly...filling your lungs to capacity...and...relax you jaw and release your breath. You are feeling more relaxed and more at peace. One more breath...in through your nose...hold...and let it go. Very good. The deep breaths are a great technique to use when you want to relax or calm down. Your entire body and mind are now feeling good and you are now going to take a trip in a car to put yourself at ease. You are driving in a convertible. This convertible can be any color you want it to be. Perhaps it is your favorite color. The convertible has soft leather seats that are very comfortable to sit in. You touch the leather. It is the softest material you have ever touched. You sink into the cushy seats. You can be driving by yourself or perhaps you have a companion, it doesn't matter. You are driving north in California. The Pacific Ocean is to your left and mountains are to your right. The road you are driving on is very curvy around the hills. You can't see very far in front of you because of the many sharp turns. You enjoy these turns, they relax you. Below and to you left you see the water from the ocean slapping against the rocks on the coast. The water is dark blue and choppy, but you don't care about the water. You are enjoying your ride; it is very relaxing. You hear the sound of your engine. It purrs slightly and has a very soothing sound. You can hear the different sounds it makes when you press harder on the accelerator or touch the brake. You are on a sort of autopilot when you drive. It comes very easy to you and you find driving very relaxing. You look to the ocean again and you can smell the salt in the air. This smell is also soothing. It smells fresh and clean. The air is untouched by smog and pollution. It feels good as you take a deep breath in, filling your lungs with the salty air. You continue to drive on the long winding road. The surface of the road is very smooth. The lanes are wide. You do not pass any cars going the opposite direction. It is just you out on this road. You enjoy taking time to yourself, driving along. You are at peace and enjoying yourself. Take time to notice the scenery. The rolling hills to your right are beautiful. There is a lot of variation in the hills. Some are steep and some form plateaus. There are many turns off the road that lead to parks. You take a look at the trees. They are tall and magnificent. You turn your eyes back to the road. You have driven many miles and you have many more miles to drive. You take a look up at the sky. You see big puffy clouds moving from your right to your left. They are moving pretty quickly. There seem to be three big clouds with a few small ones. They change shape as they move. You try to see if you can make out any shapes in the clouds. You decide to pull over in one of the parking and viewing areas. You recline your seat and close your eyes. As you do this you focus on relaxing every part of your body. You let your head drop on the headrest. You make no facial expressions because your muscles are completely relaxed. You let your muscles in your neck and shoulders loosen. As you do this, you allow your arms and hands to lie easily next to your body. You make sure your back is straight and you relax each vertebra on the back of your seat. You allow your abs and sides to loosen and relax. You move on to your hips, buttocks, and thighs. These are major muscles. It feels good to relax them after so many miles of sitting on them. You let your knees part just a little. And you relax your calves and all the muscles below your knees. You move your feet and ankles from side to side. That feels good after driving for so long. The feel very loose and relax now. You continue to lie in your car and relax your body. You are in a peaceful state of mind. You are enjoying yourself in the car. The soft leather feels nice against your skin. You continue to relax.

Driving Car 1 Deepening

You are driving in your car when you find yourself on top of a very steep mountain. The road goes straight down at a very large decline. I am going to count down from the number ten and as I do you are going to drive down the mountain. As you go down, you will find yourself going deeper and deeper into a state of hypnotic relaxation. Okay now...Ten...your car goes down the mountain...Nine...you are becoming more relaxed...eight...down down the road you go...Seven...deeper and deeper into relaxation...Six...feeling good as you drive down the mountain...Five...verrry relaxed...Four...feeling very good...Three...driving down...almost to the bottom of the mountain now...Two...and on the count of the next number you will be completely relaxed in a very deep state of hypnosis. One. Very good. You are at the bottom of the mountain. You are feeling extremely relaxed. Now you are ready to focus on _____ and make serious changes in your life.

Driving Car Induction 2 (West)

Okay, close your eyes. Put your mind and body at ease. Breathe in a big deep breath; filling your lungs with oxygen...hold it here...and slowly let all the air out. Good. Each deep breath that you take will further relax you. Now breathe in again, slowly...feeling your chest rise as your lungs expand. And open your mouth and relax your jaw...and release. Feel your body relax. One more time, breathe in deeply...expanding your lungs...really fill them up with air. And release it, feeling your lungs deflate. Good, you are now more relaxed and feeling good. Now I want you to picture yourself in a car. It can be any kind of car. Maybe it is your dream car or maybe it is your first car you ever had or maybe a motorcycle. It doesn't matter, but go ahead and picture it now. [pause] You are in your car or motorcycle and you are driving out west. It's a hot day, but you feel cool and comfortable. As you drive, you see the movement of the heat radiating from the asphalt. It looks as though the road is wet, but you know that this is just an obstacle illusion. You enjoy driving. Driving gives you time to zone out and just enjoy the scenery. The road you are on is long, straight, and flat. It goes on for miles in front of you and disappears into the horizon. You come up on a gas station and you decide to pull over and fill up your tank because you're not sure when the next gas station will be. You fill up your tank and go inside to pay. Inside the convenient store is a shop selling leather clothing. You immediately smell the distinct scent of leather. You walk over to a jacket and you touch it. It's suede and very soft to the touch. You linger a moment more and then you pay for your gas and get back to the road. Your surroundings are beautiful. The land around you is all shades of red, orange, and brown. There are large red land formations in the distance. You think about how the wind was able to carve the formation. The sun hits the large formation just right and is a brilliant shade of red. There doesn't appear to be any sign of life, no green grass or trees. The dirt is brown and barren and occasionally you see tumbleweeds blowing across the road. You continue to drive in peace. Occasionally a car or a truck or a motorcycle will pass by you. You have been on this road for miles and you have only seen four vehicles. You decide to turn your radio on and find a good station. You realize that there aren't many stations out here when all you can find is static. You turn the radio off and all you hear is the sound of your engine. Your engine has a soothing quality to it. You go into autopilot as you cruise down the road. You have no destination. You are just looking at what America has to offer. As you drive, you become more and more relaxed. You feel your head resting relax. Your eyes, ears, cheeks, and mouth loosen. You tighten the muscles in your neck and shoulders and then allow them to drop. You let your arms hang loosely from the steering wheel. Then you arch your back slightly, and then relax it into a comfortable position. You relax your chest and stomach and hips. You move around slightly in your seat so that your buttocks and thighs are comfortable and loose. You part your knees just a bit and relax your lower legs. You put your car on cruise control and take your ankles and feet and move them around until they are no longer stiff. Your head, back, stomach, legs, and feet feel very loose and relaxed. You enjoy driving down the road. Your mind and body are at ease.

Driving Car 2 Deepening

As you are driving on the long, straight, flat road, it begins to cool. The sun is just over the horizon now. You look at all the bright colors in the sky. There are shades of red, orange, and yellow that you have never seen before. The idea of the sun setting relaxes you. And now as I count down from ten, you are going to become more relaxed as you watch the sun go down into the horizon. Ten...the sun is setting...Nine...you are relaxing and feeling good...Eight...down, down goes the sun...Seven...deeper and deeper you go into a relaxed state...Six...feeling very good...Five...the sun has almost set...Four...you are going deeper and deeper...Three...the sun has almost disappeared...down it goes...Two...and on the count of the next number you will be in a very relaxed state and sun will be set behind the horizon. One. You are completely relaxed. You are feeling very calm and at ease. The sun is no longer in the sky. All that is left are the brilliant shades of color in the sky. You continue to relax...

Driving Car 3 Induction (across the US)

Okay. You are sitting in a very comfortable chair. Go ahead and close your eyes. Very good. Lets pause as you clear your mind of any thoughts. [pause] Now lets take 3 deep breaths. Breathe in, filling your lungs all the way. Fill them very slowly. Hold for a second. And now...release the air, letting it out through your mouth. You should feel a little more relaxed. Okay, now again, take a really big breath. Really fill up your lungs. Feel your chest raise up. And hold for a second...and let it all out slowly. Okay, you're feeling good. Now, one more deep breath. In through your nose, filling your lungs...now open your mouth and relax your jaw...and release, slowly and barely pushing the air out. Very good. You should be feeling more relaxed now. Now I am going to describe a journey for you. You are going to picture yourself in this journey and you are going to focus on relaxing. Imagine you are taking a road trip across the country. You start off on the East coast and you drive West. You are in a convertible because you want to be able to experience everything on this trip. The top is down on your convertible. It is a beautiful day. The sun is shining. There are some big white clouds in the sky. As you look up to the pretty blue sky you see and hear a group of geese. They have formed a massive V. There must be hundreds of them way up in the air. They are very loud considering how high up they are. You look back to the road and continue on your journey. The road is pretty boring, but you love seeing the countryside. You go over the Appalachian mountain range and continue on to the plains of the Midwest. There are a lot of farms. You wonder what the different crops are. You see a patch of bright yellow, far away in the distance. As you approach it, you see that it is actually a huge crop of yellow wildflowers. You are amazed at how many are there. You decide to get out of your car and walk through the flowers. You hold out your hands, brushing your hands against the strong flowers. They feel soft to the touch. You don't walk too far because you don't want to trample the flowers. You take a deep breath in as you walk back to your car. The scent in the air is very sweet. You pick a couple flowers to take with you in your car. You get back in your car and head west again. The flowers add a sweet fragrance to your car for days. The next day you end up driving through the Rockies. They are beautiful mountains. There is no wind today. The trees you pass are completely still. As you look into the sky, you see several cloud trails from airplanes. They dart across the entire sky in many different directions. When you look closely you can see the tiny little silver planes in the sky. You get back to your journey and enjoy the view. You go up and down many mountains and then the next day you reach the redwood forests of California. You get out of your car and stand next to the many redwoods. You look up and you still cannot see the very top of the trees. The trunks at the base are huge. It takes you a little while to walk around them. You decide that you need a break from your long car trip, so you lay down with a blanket on the ground. For a moment you appreciate the massive trees you are looking up at and then you close your eyes. You take a few deep breaths to relax your mind. You relax your whole body starting with your head. You relax your head; every muscle in your face loosens. You move your neck around and get it to relax. You move your shoulders up and back and let them relax. Your arms and hands are resting on your chair by your side. You begin to relax some more. It feels nice to be in the woods relaxing. You then move to your back, going through each vertebra and relaxing the muscles that support your spine. You relax your chest and stomach. You feel your steady breath rising and falling with your chest. You let your hips and buttocks relax in your chair. You move down to your thighs and relax each one. You let your knees dangle from your chair. Your shins and calves relax as you continue to relax your body. You move your feet around and point and flex your toes. This relaxes them and you are in a very peaceful state.

Driving Car 3 Deepening

As you lie there up at the redwood tree, you notice a trail of ants on the tree. I am going to count down from ten and as I do you are go to watch the ants move down the tree and you are going to relax. Ten...the ants move down, down the tree...Nine...you are going deeper into a state of relaxation...Eight...feeling good...Seven...ants march down...Six...you feel the relaxation going deeper and deeper...Five...deeper still...Four...the ants are almost to the base of the tree...Three...you are very relaxed...Two...and on the count of the next number, you are going to feel more relaxed than you ever have before. One. Very relaxed. You are in a deep state of hypnosis. You are so relaxed and you are ready to work on making positive changes to you life.

Flying 1 Induction (pyramids of Egypt)

Go ahead and get comfortable. Make sure you are in a good position to become as relaxed as possible. Go ahead and close your eyes. Take a second to relax your mind and body. [pause] Now lets take three deep breaths. Inhale...slowly...filling your lungs with air...that's it...and release...exhale slowly through your mouth. Once again...and inhale...slowly...filling your lungs with air...very good...and release...exhale slowly through your mouth. Last one...and inhale...slowly...filling your lungs with air...very nice...and release...exhale slowly through your mouth. Good, you should be feeling a little more relaxed and at ease. I want you to picture yourself with the ability to fly. Imagine you are flying over the Nile River in Egypt. Look at the water moving. You are flying toward the north and you can see the river flowing northward, just like you. You enjoy your ability to fly. You glide along at different speeds and at different altitudes. You are going fast now and all you can hear is the sound of wind blowing past your ears. You fly at a lower altitude now. You can see that along the riverbanks, the Nile is very green and lush. The river is a major source of water, and it allows a lot of vegetation to grow along the banks. Beyond the riverbank, all you can see is sandy desert for miles and miles. You swoop in a little closer and you can see beaches along the Nile. They are white sandy beaches. You also see many palm trees lining the river. You are a couple hundred feet above the ground. Now you can hear the sound of birds, nesting in the palm trees. It's a relaxing sound, the sound of birds singing joyfully as you fly along with them. You continue to glide through the air. You see houses along the riverbank. You see areas that are more densely populated than others. You see roads and schools. You swoop across the Nile and toward the desert. You can see the great pyramids from a great distance. They are very small at first and as you get closer, flying toward them, they get bigger and bigger. You circle around them from high above. Each of the pyramids four faces creates a point that points toward the sky. From the angle of the sun, each face of the pyramid appears to be a different shade of brown. The pyramids are massive as you fly closer to them. You ponder how they were built so many years ago. You slow down a little bit and reach your hand out to touch the pyramid. Your finger tips brush against the rough surface. You feel fortunate to be able to visit the pyramids by flying over them. You take a deep breath and smell the fresh air. You enjoyed your trip, flying over the Nile and seeing the Great Pyramids. This experience has relaxed you. As you continue to fly, you focus on relaxing your entire body. You put your head down so that it is facing the ground. You make sure that your spine and neck are straight and create one long line. You loosen your arms and hands next to your body. You continue to soar and relax as you do. You stretch out your legs, making them feel long, lean, and loose. You look down and see the desert. You see where the wind has created ripples in the sand. The sand is a light orange color. You can see the changes in altitude, some areas are flat and sometimes there are hills. You continue to relax your body. It is weightless and loose. You point and relax your feet and toes. You let them hang loosely from your ankles. Your entire body is at ease. Your mind feels uncluttered. You enjoy soaring through Egypt. Flying is a wonderful feeling. You continue to relax as you fly high into the sky.

Flying 1 Deepening

You are soaring in the sky like a bird and the sun is close to setting. As you watch the sun, I am going to count down from ten. As I count down from ten, you are going to watch the sun go down toward the horizon. As the sun goes down, you will become more and more relaxed. Alright now...Ten...the sun is drifting down...drifting down toward the horizon...Nine...you are relaxing as you watch the sun go down...Eight...down...down goes the sun...Seven...you are becoming very deeply relaxed...Six...deeper still...Five...the sun is halfway to setting...Four...you are becoming more and more deeply relaxed...Three...more relaxed as the sun goes down...down toward the horizon...Two...and on the count of the next number, you will feel more deeply relaxed than you have ever felt before...One...very relaxed. You are now in a very deep state of relaxation. The sun is set and your entire body and mind are in complete relaxation. You are ready to make positive changes in your life.

Steve G. Jones, M.Ed.

Flying 2 Induction (Caribbean)

As you sit in your comfortable chair, go ahead and close your eyes. Now in order to relax, take three deep breaths. In through your nose...inhale deeply...and...slowly...that's good. Hold here...and exhale...let it all out through your mouth. Very good. Another breath in...very slowly...filling your lungs to capacity...and...relax you jaw and release your breath...exhaling slowly. You are feeling more relaxed and more at peace. One more deep breath...inhale...in through your nose...hold...and exhale deeply from within...and let it go. Very good. The deep breaths are a great technique to use when you want to relax or calm down. You should be feeling a little more relaxed and a little more at ease. Now picture yourself flying. That's right. You are flying around the Caribbean Sea. Imagine flying over the many islands and taking in the view. As you fly over the islands, you notice how lush and green they are. The islands appear to have a ring of white around them, which you realize are the white sandy beaches that make up the perimeter of each island. Occasionally you see part of an island that has a rocky coast. You fly lower to one of these areas and you can hear the sound of the waves break against the rocks. This is a relaxing sound. You can see the wave rolling in toward the rocks and then it hits and the water turns white and splashes everywhere. You continue to fly across the islands. You can see the resorts on the islands. You see the long roads leading to them and the brilliant blue pools. As you fly across the Caribbean Sea, you are amazed by the colors and life in the sea. The sea is made up of many shades of blue and green. You can see many different reefs from this view. You know that the reef is teeming with life. From above, the reef appears to have colors of red and purple. You enjoy the sight as you glide through the air. You take a deep breath and enjoy the smell of the salty air. The smell relaxes you as you float down closer to the sea. You can tell where the sea is shallower and where it is deeper. The color of the water is a very light blue where it is shallow and a deep blue where it gets deeper. You can see boats riding across the water with their white lines from their wake, trailing from behind. You relax even more as you glide through the air. You enjoy every second of it. It is very peaceful and your entire body is relaxing. You can see aquatic life from your aerial view. You can see large fish near the surface of the water. You can see large schools of fish darting from every angle. You notice one large school, it is very big and it seems to create the impression that it is one large fish. You see the large school of fish darting through the water. Every now and then you see a splash which you decide are fish jumping into the air and fall back into the water. You continue to fly and enjoy your journey. As you fly, you focus on relaxing your entire body. Focusing on your head you allow the muscles in your temples to relax. That's right, all the muscles in your face loosen. Now open your mouth just a little and relax your jaw. Let all tension disappear. Roll your neck from side to side and let all the muscles in your neck and shoulders relax. Let your arms relax loosely by your side as you let them go limp. Focus on your lower back and stomach. Feel as each inch of your body relaxes. You feel good. Your upper body is now loose and relaxed. Now focus down to your hips and buttocks; all tension is released. Go further now. To your thighs; let them relax and go limp. You are very relaxed in the air. You feel the air sweep past your body. Now focus further down on your body to your knees and lower leg. Bend your knees slightly and let them relax. You move your ankles slightly so that there is no tension in them. That's right, feel all tension leave your legs. That feels good. Relax the arch of your foot and wiggle your toes. Your entire body now is relaxed. You are now more relaxed than you have ever felt before. You continue to glide through the air, your body completely at ease. You feel the warm air rush over you. You can feel the suns warm rays. It feels so good to completely unwind. You enjoy the feeling of getting rid of all tension in your body and mind. Now, you lay there in the boat very still and you continue to relax.

Flying 2 Deepening

You are soaring in the sky like an airplane and the sun is close to setting. As you watch the sun, I am going to count down from ten. As I count down from ten, you are going to watch the sun go down toward the horizon. As the sun goes down, you will become more and more relaxed. Alright now...Ten...the sun is moving down...moving down toward the horizon...Nine...you are relaxing as you watch the sun lower...very slowly down...Eight...down...down goes the sun...Seven...you are becoming very deeply relaxed...Six...deeper still...Five...the sun is halfway toward the horizon...Four...you are becoming more and more deeply relaxed...Three...more relaxed as the sun goes down...down toward the horizon...Two...and on the count of the next number, you will feel more deeply relaxed than you have ever felt before...One...very relaxed. You are now in a very deep state of relaxation. The sun is set and your entire body and mind are in complete relaxation. You are ready to make positive changes in your life.

Flying 3 Induction (US National Park)

Okay, you are going to take five deep breaths. Each deep breath is going to relax you. Alright now...breath in deeply and slowly...focusing on the consistent rise of your chest. That's good...now hold it for one second...and...slowly let it out. Don't push it...just easily and effortlessly let it out. You are feeling more relaxed now. Now again...breathe in...fill your lungs to capacity...excellent and hold...now release...feeling your shoulders go down. Three more times. And...breathe in...deep breath...hold here...and let it all out...very good. Now again...take a deep breath...inhale...slowly expanding your lungs...until you can't fill them any more...and...release the air...slowly...that feels good. Okay, once more...inhale slowly feeling your chest rise...that's good, hold...and release, letting all that air out. Feel yourself relax. You feel loose and light, it's a great feeling being relaxed. Imagine that you have the ability to fly. That's right. You can fly easily and effortlessly anywhere you want. Picture yourself flying over Glacier National Park in Montana. It's summer time and all the colors you see are bright and magnificent. You see mountains of dark hunter green trees. You see sides of mountains that are rocky with large gray boulders. You see the bright blue lakes, rivers, and creeks. It is a very pretty sight. You start flying at a high altitude above the mountains so that you get the perfect aerial view. You see mountains, fields, and lakes for as far as you can see. You then glide down to a lower altitude so that you can get a closer look. As you float down, you relax. The only sound you hear is the sound of wind sweeping past your ears. You relax as you get closer to the mountains and the beautiful view. Now picture yourself soaring above the treetops on a mountainside. You take a deep breath in to further relax and you breathe in the smell of pine. It's a delightful smell and this too relaxes you. There are a lot of pine trees and although you cannot see the ground, you know that these fragrant green trees are tall. You decrease more in altitude and you fly over a creek that is at the base of the mountain. You can see the movement of the water as it tumbles over small rocks. You think about how this creek probably starts near the top of the mountain as just a little trickle and far down into the valley, you can see where the creek is much wider and flows into a beautiful lake. You steer yourself toward the lake. The lake is like glass; it perfectly reflects the mountains that surround it. Next to this lake is a field of wildflowers. The flowers are red, yellow, and purple and very bright even from way above. You decide to soar down to the field of wildflowers. You glide one foot above the pretty flowers, as you do, you reach your hand down and brush your fingertips very gently against the blooms. You are careful not to disturb them. The flowers smell sweet and fragrant. As you continue to float above the field of flowers and the lake, you hear the sound of a bald eagle soaring above you. You stay close to the ground so that you do not disturb it. Its feathers look smooth to the touch. You enjoy flying around Glacier National Park, the view is very relaxing and you have seen a lot of interesting things today. As you float in the air, you relax your body. You relax your face and you make sure your head is parallel to the ground below. You loosen the muscles around your mouth and jaw. You align your neck with your back, looking down and making sure not to strain either part. You put your shoulders back and your arms and hands hang loosely by your side. You relax your torso as you glide through the air. Even though your legs are moving, you move them slowly and powerfully. You focus on each muscle in your legs starting with your hamstrings and quads and you move down. You are feeling very good and relaxed. Your knees are relaxed, your calves are relaxed. You allow your legs, feet, and toes to lengthen and stretch as you soar in the air. You feel very good as you relax and you continue to relax.

Flying 3 Deepening

You are soaring high above the mountains of Glacier National Park. You want to be closer to the ground. Take a look at the distance between where you are and where you want to be. I am going to count down from the number ten and as I do you are going to slowly descend down closer to the ground. As you descend closer to the ground, you will feel yourself relax more and more with every number. Okay now...Ten...down you go...floating down...Nine...relaxing further as you float down...Eight...down...down you go...Seven...deeper into a state of pure relaxation...Six...deeper still...Five...you are halfway down now...Four...relaxing even more into a deep state of relaxation...Three...feeling at peace and very calm...Two...and on the count of the next number...you will be more relaxed than you have ever been before...One...you are now completely relaxed. You are more relaxed than you have ever felt before. You are in a complete state of peace. You know look forward to making positive changes in your life.

Grassy Field 1 Induction (valley)

You are lying down and you are feeling very comfortable and at ease. Your eyes are closed. Take a few moments to completely clear your head of any thoughts [pause]. Now I want you to take 3 deep breaths. Breathe in...inhale...slowly...filling your lungs to capacity...that's good...and now...exhale...releasing the air, letting it out through your mouth. You should feel a little more relaxed. Okay...once again...take a big deep breath. Really fill up your lungs...feel your chest rise...and hold for a second...and exhale...let it all out...slowly. Excellent. Okay, one more deep breath. In through the nose, filling your lungs...now open your mouth and relax your jaw...and release, slowly and barely pushing the air out. Very good. You should be feeling a little more relaxed now. Now imagine yourself in a field. It's a large grassy field. All the grass around you is a vibrant green color. The grass is very healthy and lush. A warm breeze passes by your body. It feels good and refreshes you. You watch as the breeze causes the grass to sway. It glimmers in the sunshine and it looks like waves from the ocean. It sways back and forth, back and forth. The flowing movement of the grass relaxes you as you walk through the grassy field. You hear a hawk making sounds above you. You take a look up at the sky and you spot the brown bird soaring high. You like the sound that it makes; its call is clear and echoes off the mountain. You watch as it circles around above you. You take a look at your surroundings. You are in a valley of grass with a mountain to your left and a mountain to your right. The field where you are is pretty flat. The grass goes a little up the mountains on either side and then the face of the mountains turn to trees. The mountains are capped with snow at the very top. You wonder how tall the mountains are. You are glad that you are warm in the valley below. As you walk around in the grass, you can smell the fragrant sweet smell. You enjoy the smell of grass; there is no other smell quite like it. It smells earthy and natural. You take in a deep breath and relax as you exhale. You continue to walk and continue to relax. You decide to stop for a moment and run your fingers through the grass. The grass feels thick and healthy. It tickles your palm, as you brush your hand on the many blades of grass. You enjoy your time in the field. You take a look at all the colors around you. The grass is a vibrant green and then there is the darker green of the trees up the mountain. Further up the mountain is a grayish-purple hue of rocks and then you see the white of the snow-capped mountains. Beyond the mountains is the bright blue sky. It is a beautiful contrast to the green, grey, and white of the grass field and the snow-capped mountain. There are a few wispy clouds in the sky. They look like quick white brush strokes on a painter's canvas. As you walk through the green grassy field, you come to an area with a large comfortable blanket laying there for you. You lie down on the blanket and close your eyes. You relax your head; every muscle in your face just relaxes. You move your neck around as it loosens. You move your shoulders up and back and let them relax against the blanket. Your arms and hands are resting on the blanket by your side. You begin to relax some more. It feels nice to be in the grassy field relaxing. You then move to your back, going through each vertebra and relaxing the muscles that support your spine. You relax your chest and stomach. You feel your steady breath rising and falling with your chest. You let your hips and buttocks relax into the soft ground below. You move down to your thighs and relax each one. You let your knees part slightly and relax. Your shins and calves relax as you continue to relax your body. You move your feet around and point and flex your toes. This relaxes them and you are in a very peaceful state. Your body is completely at ease. You have nothing on your mind. You enjoy how you are feeling right now.

You continue to lay on the blanket in the peaceful grassy field relaxing...

Gras Field 1 Deepening

You now slowly sit up and open your eyes and look above at the beautiful mountain and sky. You notice the sun and all the colors on the horizon. The sky is filled with shades of red, orange, pink, and purple. You see that the sun is close to setting behind the mountain to your right. As I count from 10, the sun sets closer to the horizon and you relax deeper and deeper with every number I count. Okay...Ten...the sun goes down just a little and you feel yourself relax...Nine...you are going deeper into a state of relaxation...you see the sun lower and you are feeling at ease...Eight...deeper still...Seven...You are feeling more and more relaxed as you watch the sun go down...down...Six...you relax further into hypnosis...Five...the sun is another step closer to setting behind the mountain and you are very relaxed...Four...you relax more deeply...and...more deeply...Three...
deeper still...you watch the sun go down...down...Two...you are very relaxed and at the count of the next number you will be completely relaxed...One...you are very relaxed. You are feeling very comfortable. We will now focus on your subconscious mind to make changes and go forward.

Grassy Field 2 Induction (stream)

You are in a very comfortable place right now. Go ahead and close your. eyes. You are now going to take three deep breaths. Each breath will be deep and slow. Okay now…breathe in…inhaling slowly…very good…and…exhale…letting it all out…slowly. Again…deep breath in…expanding your chest and lungs…that's it…hold…and release…exhaling slowly through your mouth. You should feel yourself relax with each deep breath. Last one…inhale…through your nose…slowly…and…deeply…and…exhale…through your mouth…push out all the air. Very good. You should be feeling a little more relaxed now. Go ahead and take a few normal breaths. Feel your chest rise and fall. Find a steady rhythm. Your breathing is steady and consistent. Picture yourself in the plains of mid-western United States. You are in a large grassy field. All you see is grass for miles and miles in every direction. This large field that you are standing in is completely flat. It is a beautiful sight and you are complete peace while standing in the pretty field. The grass is long and thin. It comes up to your knees. You are able to easily bend over a little and run your hands through the grass. The lush grass feels soft along your palm and fingertips. As you meander in the grass, the only thing you hear is the wind sweeping past your ears. It's a very quiet place. You enjoy peace and quiet and you enjoy listening to the breeze. You take a look up at the sky. The sky is a light blue and contrasts nicely with the radiant green grass. You watch large clouds glide across the sky. You can see clouds for miles and miles in the clear blue sky. You watch as the clouds move and change shape [pause]. You focus your attention back toward the ground and walk a little ways through the grass. All the while you enjoy the beautiful weather. It's a perfect summer day. Your skin absorbs the suns warm rays and the refreshing breeze brings calmness to your body and soul. You come upon a small stream running through the field. You notice that the grass is even greener and healthier looking next to the stream. This grass must get more water and nutrients from the stream. Also, along the bank of the stream are some wildflowers. The wildflowers are white and yellow and the green grass is a nice background for the flowers. You bend over to smell the flowers. They smell fragrant and lovely. You enjoy the scent of the flowers as you take a few deep breaths. You breathe in deeply and slowly. Feel the consistent rise and fall of your chest. You are more relaxed now. You walk through some of the grass and wildflowers and you are standing right on the bank of the narrow stream. The stream is long and straight and seems to go on for miles. You can see that not only where you standing but for as far as you can see, the grass is more lush by the side of the stream. And you notice the white and yellow wildflowers continue also, for as far as you can see. You crouch down to your knees and reach your hand out to feel the temperature of the water. The water is about the same temperature as the air, warm yet refreshing. There are small round rocks in this stream. You touch one of the rocks. It is smooth to the touch. Years of water rolling over the rocks have smoothed the surface of the rocks. You bring your hand out of the water and shake off the excess water. You stand back up and stretch your back. You walk a little ways along the stream. As you do you start relaxing your body from head to toe. Your head sits loosely on your neck and shoulders. Your neck and shoulders are completely free of tension. You straighten your back and relax the muscles that support it. You relax your waist, hips, and buttocks as you walk. You feel the cool breeze sweeping across your body. You now focus on relaxing your legs. You allow your thighs to loosen with each step. You relax the muscles around your knees and you continue on to your shins and calves. You now relax your ankles by moving them around as you walk. They feel loose. You relax your feet and toes in your shoes as you walk. You feel like you are walking on a cloud. As you continue to walk in the beautiful grassy field you clear your mind and continue to relax...

Grassy Field 2 Deepening

You are standing and looking at the beautiful field and sky. You notice the sun and all the colors of the horizon just above the trees in the west. The western sky is filled with clouds in the shades of red, orange, pink, and purple. The sun is just a few minutes away from setting. As I count from 10, the sun sets closer to the tree line and you relax deeper and deeper with every number. Okay...Ten...the sun goes down...down in the sky and you feel yourself relax...deeper...and...deeper...Nine...you are going deeper into a relaxed state...you see the sun lower... and...you are feeling very good...Eight...deeper still...Seven...You are feeling more and more relaxed as you watch the sun go down...down toward the horizon...Six...you relax further into hypnosis...Five...the sun is another step closer to setting on the horizon and you are feeling very relaxed...Four...you relax deeper...Three...deeper, deeper...you watch the sun go down...down...Two...you are very relaxed and at the count of the next number you will be completely relaxed...One. You are very relaxed. Very comfortable. We will now focus on your subconscious mind to make positive changes and go forward with your life.

Grassy Field 3 Induction (tree)

Okay...you are sitting in a very comfortable chair. Go ahead and close your eyes; very good. Now go ahead and pause as you clear your mind of any thoughts [pause]. You are going to take 3 deep breaths. Breathe in...filling your lungs all the way...fill them very slowly...hold for a second...and now...exhale...release the air...letting it out through your mouth. You should be feeling a little more relaxed. Okay...now again...inhale...take a big breath...really fill up your lungs...feel your chest raise up...and hold for a second...and let it all out...slowly exhaling. Okay, you're feeling good. Now, one more deep breath...inhale through your nose...filling your lungs...now open your mouth and relax your jaw...and release, slowly and lightly pushing the air out. Very good. You should be feeling more relaxed now. Picture yourself in an area with rolling hills of green grassy fields. Imagine that you are at the bottom of one of these little hills. There are hills all around you. Most of the hills have grass, but many have trees also. The hill that you are standing on the bottom of has a large oak tree on the top. It is the only tree on this hill. It looks majestic as it towers above the hill and the surrounding area. You decide to walk up the gentle slope toward the tree. As you do, you smell the sweet smell of the grass. You enjoy the way the grass smells. It is a slight scent and it puts you at ease. You enjoy being outside with nature and you enjoy your alone time. The grass is green, with a slight hue of yellow. The blades are thin and long, reaching just below your knees. You enjoy your walk up toward the great oak tree. You stop for a moment and you can hear the tree flourishing with the sound of birds. There are many different singing birds. You try to make out what kind of birds they are. You can't quite figure it out, but they do sound happy. You continue on your walk and you enjoy listening to the joyful sounds of the songbirds. You look at the entire tree now. You realize just how big the trunk is. The oak tree has thousands of branches, each getting smaller the farther away it is from the trunk. The tree is very impressive. You think to yourself how old the tree is. You wonder what it has seen in its lifetime. You walk up to the trunk and examine the bark. The bark is rough on your palm and fingertips. The bark looks to be a brownish-grey color. The circumference of the tree is longer than your arm span. You take a step back and take a look up through the branches. The suns rays are barely able to reach the ground below the tree through the maze of branches. You see on the other side of the tree that there is a swing attached to one of the low-lying branches. Two thick ropes come down from the branch and they are connected, a few feet from the ground, by a board. The swing is swaying very gently in the light breeze. You decide to sit on the swing and you do so easily and gracefully. You pump your legs lightly as you move up and down on the swing. As you swing you focus on relaxing your entire body. You lean your head and neck back in a comfortable position. Your shoulders and arms relax as you hold lightly onto the ropes with your hands. You relax each vertebra in your back…one…by…one. Your stomach and your sides are loose. Your hips and thighs rest easily on the board of the swing. You feel light and comfortable as you swing back and forth…back and forth. You stretch out your legs…all the way to your toes. Your legs feel light and airy as you continue to swing. You close your eyes and relax your mind. You clear your head of all thoughts. You are at peace swinging on the swing…attached to a strong and sturdy branch…under a magnificent tree…on a green grassy hill…in a beautiful area. You continue to relax and enjoy yourself as you swing back and forth…

Grassy Field 3 Deepening

You are sitting still on a comfortable swing under a large oak tree. You look out into the distance, on the horizon, and you see the fiery sun hovering over the treetops. The sun has cast an orangey glow on the hill and there are beautiful red clouds throughout the sky. You watch as it is about to set. I am going to count down from ten and as I do, the sun is going to set lower and lower. As the sun goes down, you are going to relax more and more deeply. Okay now...Ten...down goes the sun...closer to setting now...Nine...deeper and deeper you go into a deep state of relaxation...Eight...you watch as the sun sets down...down toward the tree tops...Seven...you are going deeper now...relaxing more and more...Six...deeper still...Five...feeling at ease as the sun goes down...further...and...further...Four...you continue to relax as the sun moves closer to the horizon...Three...deeper and deeper you go...Two...and on the count of the next number...you are going to be in a very deep state of relaxation...One...you are completely relaxed. You are feeling more relaxed than you have ever felt before. Your mind and body are completely peaceful and at ease. You are ready to make positive changes to your life.

Home 1 Induction (country)

Okay, close your eyes. Put your mind and body at ease. Take in a deep breath...inhale...filling your lungs with air...and hold it here...and let it all out slowly. Good. Each deep breath that you take will help relax you. Now breathe in again...deeply...and...slowly...feeling your chest rise. And open your mouth and relax your jaw...and release. Feel your body relax. One more time, breathe in deeply...expanding your lungs...really fill them up with air. And...exhale...release the air...feeling your lungs deflate. Good, you are now more relaxed and feeling good. Go ahead and close your eyes if you haven't already. Imagine you are on a large piece of land. You own this land and it consists of 100 acres. In the middle of this property is a house; this is your house. You are standing in your long driveway. This driveway is made of dirt and stones. Surrounding your driveway are rolling hills of grass and wildflowers. In the distance you see a wooded area; that is part of your property too. On top of one of the hills, you see one large oak tree. As you look closely, you see two ropes hanging from a branch and at the bottom of these ropes, is a board. The ropes and board create a swing. You walk off your driveway and into the long grassy field. As you walk, you point your fingertips away from your body and you let the tips of the grass brush along the tips of your fingers. The feeling against your fingertips relaxes you. You stop for a moment and take a look up into the big sky. The sky is bright blue with large white fluffy clouds moving from west to east. You watch the clouds as they slowly move across the sky. They change a little in shape. You try to see if any of the clouds take a recognizable shape, but right now you can't make out anything. You continue to stand in the field of grass, watch the clouds float across the sky. This moment relaxes you. You feel calm and peaceful. You walk back to the driveway and then take a detour to the front steps. As you walk up the steps, you hear the sound of a cat meowing. You look down and the cat is rubbing its body against your leg. You lean down to pet it. As you pet the kitty, you feel the purring vibrations against your fingertips. The outdoor cat has an orange coat with stripes of light orange and dark orange. You leave the cat to bask in the sunlight and you walk into your house. The floors of the house are wooden and well worn in. You walk by a large wooden staircase and turn to your right into the kitchen. You smell the delicious smell of home baked cookies in the oven. You turn around and walk up the staircase. There are three bedrooms upstairs. You walk into your bedroom. There is a large bed in the middle of the room. The window is open and the sheer linen drape is blowing in the breeze. Your room is almost all white. The walls are white, although they have turned off-white through the years. Your bedspread is white. You decide to lie down for a little while and rest your feet. You turn the sheets down and climb inside. You let your head lay on the fluffy white pillow. You close your eyes and feel your body release all tension. Your neck and back sink into the mattress and each vertebra is at ease. You lay your arms and hands by your side on top of the bedspread. You let your hips and buttocks sink into the mattress as well. You tighten both your legs and then allow all tension to release until they feel light as air. You let your feet fall to the side and relax. It feels good to no longer be standing on them. You lay in bed, fully awake, but relaxing your entire body and mind. Your mind is clear of all thoughts. You enjoy this peaceful time to yourself. You lay there in your comfortable bed, in your white room, in your old house, on your beautiful land. And you continue to relax…

Home 1 Deepening

You are in the beautiful house on the grassy hilltop. You are in a hallway on top of a heavy wooden staircase. The wood is made of beautiful mahogany. You put your hand on the banister and feel the smoothness of the wood. You look down the stairs and you see ten steps. You see where the wood is more worn at the center of each step from years of wear and tear. I am going to count down from ten. As I count down from ten, you are going to take a step down. As you take a step down, you are going to relax into a deeper state with each step. You're holding on to the banister...Ten...down one step...Nine...another step down...feeling more relaxed...Eight...feeling more deeply relaxed...Seven...deeper still...Six...feeling more and more relaxed as you take another step down...down the beautiful staircase...Five...halfway down the stairs...becoming more and more relaxed...Four...deeper now into a state of relaxation...Three...down...down the stairs...Two...and on the count of the next number you are going to be more relaxed than you have ever been before...One...completely relaxed. Your entire body and mind are very peaceful and more relaxed that you have ever felt. You are ready to make positive changes in your life.

Steve G. Jones, M.Ed.

Home Induction 2 Induction (beach house)

Go ahead and get in a comfortable position...close your
eyes. That's good. Now you are going to take three deep
breaths. On each one you are going to concentrate on
filling your lungs with air very slowly each time. Alright
now...inhale...breathing   deeply...and
slowly...and...exhale...releasing all air through your
mouth...very   good...again...inhale...through   your
nose...pause...and...exhale...out through your mouth.
Last deep breath right here...inhale...slowly...deeply...feel
your   chest   rise...and...exhale...slowly...through   your
mouth. Very good. This should have helped you relax a
little more. Now for a moment, focus on your steady and
consistent normal breaths. [pause]. Picture yourself on a
beach. You are packing your towel up and your other
things. You brush the sand off your body. You look up at
the brilliant yellow sun and you are wondering what time it
is. You look out into the sea. The sun is glistening off the
water. You see pelicans gliding just inches away from the
surface of the ocean. You see and hear sea gulls darting
overhead. There is no one on the beach right now. You
have the beach all to yourself. Behind you is your beach
house. You peer up at it. It's a yellow house with white
shutters. You have a screened in porch in the back. That is
where you enjoy spending most of your time. You gather
your things and climb the steps onto the boardwalk. The
boardwalk is several feet above the dunes and leads to
your house. The wood feels warm against your feet as you
walk along. On the edge of the dunes are sea oats; they
are swaying in the breeze. You continue to walk along the
boardwalk when you notice little sand crabs scurrying into
holes in the dunes. You enjoy watching them move
sideways in the sand. You walk down some steps and into
your backyard. There are 20 stepping-stones leading to

your back porch. You step from one stone to the next. You look up at the clear blue sky and see some small puffy clouds here and there. They seem to be standing completely still as if there was no wind way up in the sky. As you approach the door to your porch, you smell the fragrant scent of roses. Lining your back porch you have dozens of rose bushes. They are in bloom with all sorts of different color buds. There are deep crimson roses, peach roses, yellow roses, and delicate white tea roses. You breathe in the aromatic scent until it fills your lungs. You step in front of your door and brush your feet off. You reach your hand out to the shiny gold doorknob and turn it. The knob feels smooth and cool to the touch. You walk in, close the door and put your things down. With a flip of a switch you put on some music. The sound of music fills the air and makes you feel at ease. You enjoy one song after the other. In the corner of your screened in porch, you have a hammock. You walk over to the hammock and easily climb in. You feel the gentle breeze come through the screens and brush across your body. The breeze is refreshing and calms you. You have a small pillow beneath your head and you close your eyes. You say back and forth…back and forth…feeling the warm breeze against your body. You feel like you are floating on the cloud you saw earlier. You feel as light as air. You now focus on relaxing your entire body. You start with your head. You relax the muscles in your face and in your jaw. That's good. Moving down to your neck and shoulders, you relax every muscle. Feel all tension release. Your arms, hands, and fingers lay loosely by your side as you sway on the hammock. Focus on relaxing your core, your lower back, sides, and abs. Now moving further down your body, to your hips and buttocks, you relax these muscles even more. That feels good doesn't it? Relax your thighs. Relax your knees. Relax your calves and shins. Your legs are now completely lifeless. Move down to your ankles, feet, and toes. There is no tension in your feet. Your entire body is now very relaxed. Enjoy this relaxation. Now focus on relaxing your mind. You do not cloud your brain with random thoughts. You focus on relaxing further and enjoying swaying in the hammock. You enjoy this feeling; the feeling of total relaxation of your body and mind.

Home Induction 2 Deepening

Now picture yourself at the end of the boardwalk on top of stairs, next to the dunes, that leads you down to the beach. It's a staircase with 10 steps. There is a sturdy railing to either side. The steps are sturdy too. You hold on to the railing with one hand. I am going to count down from ten and as I count, you will take a step down. With each step that you take...you will become more and more relaxed. Ten...you go down one step...that's right...feel yourself relax...Nine...you take another step down...down...relaxing further... Eight...becoming more and more deep in a state of hypnosis...Seven...becoming even more relaxed with each step...feeling good...Six...deeper and deeper as you go down. Five...another step down...feeling more relaxed. Four...down a step...deeply into a relaxed state and three...further down...down...Two...and on the count of the next number you will be completely relaxed...One...you are completely relaxed and feeling good. You are in a deeper state of relaxation than you have ever been before. You are ready to make positive changes in your life.

Steve G. Jones, M.Ed.

Home 3 Induction (mountain home)

Okay now. You are lying down in a very comfortable place. I want you to close your eyes. Go ahead and relax your body. In order to better relax, I want you to take three deep breaths. Okay, now inhale...through your nose...a really deep breath...and hold...and release...exhale...good. Another deep breath in...fill your lungs with air...keep expanding them slowly...and hold...and let your mouth open and exhale...feeling your chest fall. Excellent, you should be feeling more relaxed. Now one last deep breath...inhale through your nose...expand your lungs letting your chest rise...good...and exhale...let it all out slowly. Very good. Your mind is completely clear of any thoughts. You are in a quiet place and it is now time to relax even more. You are standing outside of your mountain home. You own ten acres of land on top of a mountain. Beautiful spruce, fir, and pine trees surround your home. As you look at all the trees around you, you notice all the snow sitting on them. It has snowed a good amount today. You are standing in your driveway, bundled up in your winter jacket. You have just finished shoveling the snow off your driveway. You take a look at your house. You love your house. It's green and tan and normally blends in perfectly with the trees around it, but with the white snow as a backdrop, your home stands out. As you walk down your driveway toward your house, a brown rabbit hops across the driveway and disappears into the bushes. He was a small rabbit with large ears and a furry brown coat. You walk up to your front stoop and bang any excess snow off your boots. You walk inside and sit down in a chair you have next to your front door. You bend down and take off your boots. Your toes are cold and you look forward to warming them up. You walk through your house, warming your toes on the plush carpet. You walk to the opposite side of your house where you have a large cozy room with huge windows that allow you to take in the beautiful view. First, you walk over to the large stone fireplace and start a fire. You have done this countless times, so the process of starting a fire is easy and takes little effort. You watch as the small branches take the fire, then the large logs. The flame is blue near the bottom, then red, and then orange flames seem to climb through the air up the chimney. You feel the warm heat emitting from the fireplace. You take a deep breath in and breathe in the smell of the fire. This smell puts you at ease. The smoky scent fills your lungs and relaxes you. You grab a large blanket from a nearby basket and wrap it around your body. The blanket feels soft and smooth against your skin. You sit down on your window seat and enjoy the beautiful view as you warm up with the blanket and fire. Your house is at the top of a large mountain. There are other mountains all around you. Because of the snow, the trees appear white. You can see smoke curling up into the air on a neighboring mountain. Someone else is keeping warm from their fireplace. You hear a sound outside a window. You know what the sound is before you see it; the sound of a small airplane circling the mountains. You hear it for a while before you see it because it is echoing off the neighboring mountain. You then see the yellow airplane. You guess that it seats four people, including the pilot. The airplane soon disappears along with the muffled sound of its engine. You lay back on your window seat. You are feeling warm inside and out now. You lay your head on a pillow and focus on relaxing your body. Your head and neck rest easily and effortlessly on the pillow. You ease your shoulders and back as they relax on the cushion of the window seat. You feel a wave of warmth and peace rush over you. You continue to allow your stomach, hips, and buttocks relax as you lay down. You stretch out your legs; they feel long and lean. You relax each muscle in your legs, one by one. You let your knees and feet fall slightly to your sides. You are feeling very relaxed. Your toes are now warm and you are feeling very good. You continue to lie there relaxing every inch of your body.

Home 3 Deepening

You are feeling very relaxed. And now you are about to become even more relaxed. You are laying on your window seat, looking out your window at the surrounding snow and trees. You are laying there and you look up at the sky. You see that it is starting to snow. You focus on one snowflake way up in the sky. I am going to count down from ten and as I do, you are going to watch that snowflake fall. As the snowflake falls closer to the ground, you are going to become more and more relaxed. Alright now...Ten...the snowflake is falling down...down...Nine...you are becoming more relaxed now...Eight...down...down falls the snow...Seven...deeper and deeper you relax...more deeply relaxed...Seven...deeper still...Six...the snow keeps falling...closer and closer to the ground...Five...you are relaxing more and more...Four...you are relaxing deeper and deeper as the snow falls...the snow falls down...down...Three...the snowflake is getting closer to the ground and you relax...deeper...and...deeper...Two...and on the count of the next number, you will be more relaxed than you have ever felt before...One...Alright now. You are completely relaxed. You are in a state of pure relaxation. You are now ready to work on making positive changes to your life.

Answers to Questions in Chapters

One and Two

Chapter 1 - Inductions

Question 1 answer:
Possible answer:
> As you walk along the beach, you can feel the warm, soft, powdery sand under your feet.

Question 2 answer:
Possible answer:
> You can smell the fresh, salty, ocean breeze.

Question 3 answer:
Possible answer:
> You can see the birds off in the distance above the blue ocean water.

Question 4 answer:
Possible answer:
> You can hear the waves as they gently roll onto the shore.

Question 5 answer:
> Because the subconscious mind takes words literally. Therefore, you must make sure that what the client hears is the correct pronunciation of each word so that they do mistake one word for another.

Chapter 2: Deepenings

Question 1 answer:
> Relaxation.

Question 2 answer:
> Chest for breathing. Head, neck and hands for pulse.

Question 3 answer:
> One set is enough.

Question 4 answer:
> No. Keep it in just to be sure of their depth of trance.

Appendix

I have over two decades of experience in hypnosis. I have a Bachelor of Science degree from the University of Florida, an M.Ed. from Armstrong Atlantic State University, and I am working on a doctorate degree at Georgia Southern University. I am a certified clinical hypnotherapist, a member of both the American Board of Hypnotherapy and the National Guild of Hypnotists, president of the American Alliance of Hypnotists, and director of the Steve G. Jones School of Hypnotherapy. I am also on the board of directors of the American Lung Association in Los Angeles. I currently live in Savannah, Georgia, but I see clients and teach classes worldwide.

My client base consists largely of people who need to lose weight or gain confidence. Other clients include sales teams interested in boosting motivation and increasing income, singles searching for love, insomniacs desiring proper sleep, and smokers wanting to change their habits, to name just a few topics.

It is my hope that this book will create a cadre of hypnotherapists who feel a strong commitment toward practicing with integrity, thus altering negative perceptions about hypnotherapy, while allowing people to make positive changes. To this end, I am providing you with the tools to change people's habits and perceptions, and to help them overcome fears. I know that you can help your patients find love, make a fortune, and reach their optimum level of physical fitness through hypnotherapy.

For more information about me and about hypnotherapy, I invite you to visit my website, www.stevegjones.com. There, you will find a collection of hypnotherapy CDs, mp3s, and audio books. Among the recorded sessions, you will find over 120 titles including

Weight Loss, Unlimited Motivation, and Unlimited Confidence.

You also will find a link to my e-mail address, steve@stevegjones.com. I am available to answer your questions or address your concerns, and I wish you all the luck and prosperity the world has to offer.

Client Form

**Use the form on the following page to keep track of
your sessions.**

Steve G. Jones, M.Ed.

Record Sheet

NAME:_____

SESSION NUMBER	DATE	INDUCTION	DEEPENING	SCRIPT	COMMENTS

Steve G. Jones, M.Ed.

References

Bierman, S. (1995). Medical hypnosis. *Advances: The Journal of Mind-Body Health, 11*(1), 65.

Blakeslee, S. (2005). 3, 2, 1:This Is Your Brain Under Hypnosis. *New York Times, 155*(53406), F1-F4.

Complementary and Alternative Medicine. (2004). *Southern Medical Journal*

Resources

Steve G. Jones, M.Ed., Clinical Hypnotherapist
(The official website of Steve G. Jones)

http://www.stevegjones.com

American Alliance of Hypnotists
(Membership is free in this worldwide online directory)

http://www.hypnotistsalliance.com

Classes on Hypnotherapy
(Become a certified clinical hypnotherapist online in eight weeks)

http://americanallianceofhypnotists.org/classes.htm

Hypnotherapy pre-recorded sessions
(Over 250 specific topics such as weight loss on CD and mp3)

http://www.stevegjones.com/products.htm

Hypnotherapy Scripts
(Mostly written by MD's and Ph.D.'s)

Hammond, D. Corydon. *Handbook of Hypnotic Suggestions and Metaphors*. 1990. New York: W. W. Norton and Company. (A Norton Professional Book from the American Society of Clinical Hypnosis.)

Books by Steve G. Jones, M.Ed.
Available at http://www.stevegjones.com/books.htm
and select bookstores worldwide.

-Basic Hypnotherapy for Professionals

-Advanced Hypnotherapy for Professionals

-Hypnotherapy Inductions and Deepenings Volume I

-Hypnotherapy Inductions and Deepenings Volume II

-Hypnotherapy Scripts Volume I

-Hypnotherapy Scripts Volume II

-Hypnotic Techniques for Dating Success

-Business guide for Hypnotherapists (Office set-up, websites, forms, advertising online, search engine optimization, creating and selling hypnotherapy CD's and mp3's)

-Hypnotic Sales Mastery Techniques

-Hypnosis for Laymen

-Past Life Regression Hypnotherapy

-Hypnotherapy Case Studies